How To
ANALYZE
POETRY

CHRISTOPHER RUSSELL REASKE

DEPARTMENT OF ENGLISH
HARVARD UNIVERSITY

A MONARCH BOOK
PUBLISHED by PRENTICE HALL PRESS
NEW YORK, NY 10023

A Monarch Book
Published by Prentice Hall Press
A Division of Simon & Schuster, Inc.
Gulf+Western Building
One Gulf+Western Plaza
New York, NY 10023

PRENTICE HALL PRESS and MONARCH
PRESS are trademarks of Simon & Schuster, Inc.

Manufactured in the United States of America

11   12   13   14   15   16   17   18   19   20

ISBN: 0-671-18747-3

CONTENTS

INTRODUCTION

THE PURPOSE OF ANALYSIS: Analyzing poetry is an activity which has concerned many readers for many years. It is a given assumption that it is worthwhile. We take that leap of faith because we have found that analyzing poetry is an enjoyable and provocative mental exercise. Basically we are concerned here with explaining the methods and techniques of taking a poem apart in order to arrive at a greater understanding of both its construction and its meaning.

THE APPARATUS OF ANALYSIS: Like any apprentice tradesmen, those of us who want to analyze poetry skillfully must first become familiar with our tools. Actually, we have more of them at our disposal than the novice might suspect. In the early chapters of this book we will survey our tools and then, in subsequent chapters, carefully apply them to well-known poems. Through the example of the analysis of these poems it is hoped that one will be able to approach any poem sensibly, and then imaginatively arrive at an enlarged understanding of precisely what kind of poem it is and, ultimately, whether or not it is to be considered a good poem.

The names of tools are important. Before we can talk about *irony*, *didacticism*, or *paradox*, we first need to know precisely what these terms mean. Furthermore, it is essential that we be able to discuss the *versification* of a poem. That is, what can we say about a poem in a purely mechanical sense? How long are the lines? What kind of rhyme does it exhibit, etc.? Once we have completely familiarized ourselves with the tools, actual analysis will prove much easier than one might think.

WHAT ANALYSIS LOOKS FOR: Many people share a belief in the incorrect notion that analyzing poetry is somehow vague or even "far-out." Nothing could be further from the truth. For there is a great deal of concrete information to be presented when discussing a poem. Granted, one should be imaginative in explaining a poem's possible but less obvious meanings. But first, it is important to be able to tell the reader the most essential "facts" about the poem. It has a definite *mood* or *atmosphere*; it is written from a particular *point of view*; it can be *concrete* or *abstract*, *sarcastic* or *serious*, *tragic* or *comic*, *ironic* or *literal*, etc. The point is that there are specific things that not only can be said about a poem but even *need* to be said. It would be useless to begin talking about possible meanings of a poem, for example, before even acquainting the reader with whether or not the poem rhymes or even, in a simpler sense, whether it is a long poem or a short poem. In other words, every poem can be analyzed, to a certain extent, in a completely methodical fashion. To illuminate possible methods is the purpose of this book. It is not designed to transform the reader into an expert critic, but rather to help the student unfamiliar with poetic analysis toward an appreciation for, and skill in, the methods of analysis.

DIFFERENT POEMS REQUIRE DIFFERENT APPROACHES: It is important to realize that there is a large variety of ways in which one can discuss poetry. Different poems, or different kinds of poems, must be approached in different ways. No one could accurately or usefully analyze Coleridge's "The Rime of the Ancient Mariner" in the same way that one would analyze Frost's "Stopping by Woods on a Snowy Evening." By considering case examples of analysis we will see how to make the method best fit the poem in question, that is, how to decide which key to use for a particular lock.

FORM AND CONTENT: All literary material has both form and content. A poem, in other words, will have both a basic structure and a particular experience to relate. There is a strong, if perhaps not always clearly definable, relationship between content and form, or between subject-matter and technique. There are various kinds of poetic forms which describe not only the whole poem but its various parts as well. The content of a poem in recent times has come to mean the "experience" which the poem crystallizes or distills. Many experiences are basic to the poetry of all time—we think immediately, for example, of the experiences of love and death.

DICTION AND VERSIFICATION: The irreducible content of a poem is of course the collections of *words*. Each word in a poem is *selected* for a particular reason, often because of its various connotations or implications. There must be a resulting *suggestiveness* produced by the words themselves. The ways in which the words are arranged and made to rhyme (or not to rhyme, for let us dispel at once the incorrect notion that all poetry rhymes) leads us to *versification*, which is the art of metrical composition, the putting together of words to make poems (a poet was originally called a "makar" or "maker"). Certain repeated patterns of versification create relationships between one poem and another and sometimes between poets. If a large number of good poets *versify* in a similar way, they are usually referred to as a *school* of poets. The "Metaphysical School" of poetry, for example, binds together such poets as Donne, Vaughan, Herbert, and Marvell. The "Romantic School" of poetry links Wordsworth and Coleridge to Shelley and Keats. And so forth. In the history of English poetry, certain proven forms, and certain proven subjects, have endured. When a certain kind of poetry ceases to be entertaining to the readers of an era, it dies and awaits a "revival" (which sometimes of course never comes).

THE LIMITS OF ANALYSIS: There is virtually no limitation placed on the analysis of poetry. One can go quite "far" when trying to arrive at the meaning of a poem. One reaches a point where one can not find evidence for proving what the poet meant when he wrote certain lines. One then has to be resourceful, to use the imagination, and, in particular, to search for the least obvious, yet possible, meaning. Often the bizarre leads to the correct, just as one's very first ideas about a poem are often the most significant and profound. Interpreting a poem is sometimes a matter of "intuition"—making the difference between cut-and-dry explication, and imaginative interpretation. However, it would be wrong to decide that analyzing poetry is all guesswork or "playing hunches." The good reader asks more of himself—or, at least, as much of himself as he asks of the poet. When T. S. Eliot or Shakespeare wrote enigmatic lines of poetry they quite explicitly hoped to awaken our curiosity, and arouse us into creative thought.

THE MANY TYPES OF POETRY: We should understand at the outset that poetry can be written for different reasons and therefore each poem has a different purpose. Some poems are written purely to entertain us, others solely for the purpose of moral persuasion. We are urged perhaps to right action—or perhaps to wrong action. We are tempted—or told to resist temptation. Many poems try to be both entertaining and instructive, both amusing and edifying at the same time. Whenever we analyze a poem, we must consider, as best we can, the purposes the poet had in writing it.

POINTS OF VIEW: It may be that we will judge a poem unsuccessful because it does not accomplish the poet's announced or obvious purpose. At the same time, however, we may decide that the poem is nevertheless successful when considered from some other point of view. But it is very important that we always explain this distinction. If we were to praise a poem without explaining that we were doing so in spite of the author's failure to accomplish what he had outlined for himself, it would be assumed that we were misreading the poem, or perhaps "missing the point." At every step in poetic analysis, we must be sure that we are letting our reader know precisely what we are discussing and why. How futile it would be to explain carefully the disease imagery of *Hamlet* without saying why we are even interested in this particular imagery pattern, or without suggesting reasons for Shakespeare's use of these patterns.

THE CRITIC: This discussion about judging a poem *for the right reasons* leads us to consider momentarily what we mean by "critic." Some people wrongly assume that a "critic" of poetry criticizes poems—that is, says harsh things about them. A "critic" is simply one who reads and attempts to explain poetry. One could offer only the highest praise for a poet or a poem and be an excellent "critic." Being a critic, in short, is being a creative and conscientious reader; one reads carefully, ferreting out meaning, surveying and understanding the basic design or form of the poem, and then writes down all of his collected information in a lucid and helpful fashion. The critic, in other words, is anyone who is willing to make some comment on a poem. This comment, or criticism, could range from an "I like it" statement to a one-thousand-page detailed analysis of one stanza. But again, let us remember that anyone who attempts to analyze poetry, no matter how skillfully, is a critic.

TWO LEVELS OF MEANING: THE LITERAL AND THE SYMBOLIC:
When we talk about analyzing poetry, we must always bear in mind the basic two-fold approach of all of our reading of poetry: we must understand both the literal sense of the poem and the symbolic or suggested meaning of the poem. It is, further, important to understand the nature of the relationship between the different "levels" of a poem's "meaning." There will of course be more agreement with regard to basic literal meaning. To further possible "hidden" meanings we all bring different psychological backgrounds and associations. A word like "slaughter," for example, might have very different connotations when presented to different audiences.

THE VARIETY OF THE READERS' RESPONSE: *Poetic Responsiveness.* No poem is ever completed. By this we mean that the poet always leaves some work for his reader. A poem only prompts us, stimulates us to further consideration. How, for example, could any poem say everything there is to be said about death? Certainly more poetry has been devoted to the feelings of love than to any other feeling—and yet they of course remain basically undefined. Because of this general incompletion, none of us who criticizes poetry can be all wrong. True, we may wander too far from the intention of the poem, but as long as we make *some* response, we are functioning as critics. Being critics entails making some sort of judgement about the value and purposes of works of literature. One reader's judgement may cause another reader to express dissent—and this is usually desirable. If Dr. Johnson, for example, had not been so harsh in his judgement of Milton's "Lycidas," the poem would never have received the proper kind of rigorous analysis later given to it. Dissent, in other words, often leads to discovery.

GRASPING THE CENTRAL IMAGE: When we analyze anything —in our case poetry—we always begin by separating it into its component parts. This done, we try to examine each of the parts first separately, then in relationship to each other, and, finally, in relationship to the whole. For in poetry things have a great dependency on each other; sometimes, once we have taken a poem apart, we suddenly understand the central image and then we understand quickly all of the other parts. Analysis, in other words, is a process of intellectual dissection of a whole into its ingredients in order to understand and appreciate the integrity and meaning of the whole—the poem.

DISCOVERING THE POET IN THE POEM: One reason we undertake the analysis of poetry is to discover what is "characteristic" of a particular poet. If we consistently find the poet using a certain kind of image, or writing lines of a certain number of "poetic feet," we will eventually be able to make some supportable generalizations about his poetry on the whole. Usually as we labor toward what is characteristic we need to make trial hypotheses, find exceptions, then move on to new hypotheses. Hopefully we will ultimately be led to an understanding of the technique of the poet and a valid judgement about his work.

POETRY AND LIFE: To become appreciative readers of poetry, in any case, it is necessary that we work for both concrete and subtle analysis of the poems we read. If we make no effort to understand in various ways, we can not consider ourselves good readers. As Ben Jonson advised his readers in an epigram: "Pray thee, take care, that tak'st my book in hand,/To read it well: that is, to understand." As readers like Matthew Arnold and T. S. Eliot have repeatedly pointed out, we arrive at a greater understanding of people and of our society by arriving at an understanding of poetry; there is indeed a relationship between "the literature we read and the life we lead."

POETRY AS ART: In directing our attention to the problem of responding correctly to a poem's meaning, we perhaps have neglected the question of responding to its art. For no poem is ever detached from its aesthetic presentation. It is not as easy to respond to art as one might think, but we must confront the art of writing poetry *as* an art. First of course we must eliminate some of our presuppositions about certain kinds of *form*. If we have decided in advance that we do not enjoy unrhymed poetry, we are not going to pass intelligent or useful judgement on the next unrhymed poem that we read. To replace prejudice with skillful appreciation is a constant endeavor. And if we must ultimately conclude that a certain kind of artistic expression is *bad*, let us at least so decide for the *right* reasons.

As with meaning, art operates on different levels. There is the basic art—metrical composition—which is the foundation for any poem. Even if it is missing, it is basic *because* it is missing. We always need to begin with the elements of this foundation and thus in the first chapter we will turn to basic versification—the principles of meter, rhyme, and rhythm. The art of using words to make a poem—diction, tone, imagery—operates upon this basic foundation.

There is a higher kind of aesthetic interest attached to any poem. This art resides in the intellectual fulfillment of our aesthetic needs. The art of any poem can either *satisfy* our senses or *disappoint* them. There should be a balance between the intellectual experience which the poem leads us to expect and the fulfillment of those expectations—a resolution of the tension of the poetic experience. If the subject matter seems to require an abstract artistic presentation but is instead given a concrete one, we naturally react to the disparity between the experience the poem leads us to expect, and the actual presentation. We leave the poem with the sincere wish that the poet had presented his idea differently. In short, then, we must be willing to pass judgement on this higher artistic expression which we search for (sometimes futilely) consciously or unconsciously, in every poem we read.

There are certain basic literary conventions which we recognize in the realm of art and the more important of these are explained in Chapter 3. We are really engaged in the art of analyzing poetry as long as we respond to both the content and the art of a poem, dissecting it into its various parts, all in the effort of arriving at a greater understanding of the poem, the poet, poetry, and life. Notice that we say the *art* of analyzing poetry. Let us agree from the beginning that the analysis of poetry calls for responding to art with art. Analysis itself can be as bad as the worst of poems—or as good as the best. Analysis is self-conscious—but so is the composition of poetry. Analysis is comprehensive—but so is a poem. And in learning to practice the art of analyzing poetry, let us pursue a goal of excellence. Only then will the poets be satisfied.

BASIC VERSIFICATION

INTRODUCTION: Versification is the study and analysis of the structure of verse. It is in this area of examination that our "tools" for analyzing poetry are most specific and definitive. Versification is the study of what is most basic to a poem—its technical framework and pattern of construction.

RHYTHM AND METRICS

RHYTHM IN POETRY: Rhythm in poetry is created by the patterns of repeated sounds—in terms of both duration and quality —and ideas. We will begin our investigation of versification with a discussion of *accent*; when stress is placed on a word, accent results. But before we do this, the reader should try to "feel" the accent as it creates a rhythm. If we read some stanzas from Coleridge's "The Rime of the Ancient Mariner," for example, we immediately should hear the rhythm:

> The sun came up upon the left,
> Out of the sea came he!
> And he shone bright, and on the right,
> Went down into the sea.
>
> Higher and higher every day,
> Till over the mast at noon—
> The Wedding-Guest here beat his breast,
> For he heard the loud bassoon.
>
> The bride hath paced into the hall,
> Red as a rose is she;
> Nodding their heads before her goes
> The merry minstrelsy.

> The Wedding-Guest he beat his breast,
> Yet he cannot choose but hear;
> And thus spake on that ancient man,
> The bright-eyed Mariner.

The patterns of sound have an enchanting effect. The accent and the final sound of the second line in the third stanza, "Red as a rose is she," echoes the second line in the first stanza, "Out of the sea came he!" The general proliferation of "ee" sounds, and the repetition of the words *Wedding-Guest* and *breast* contribute equally to the flowing sound of the poem, and the chanting effect of internal rhyme. The point is that rhythm is created out of the patterned use of various words, sounds, and accents which establish in our minds a collection of associations of sound and meaning. Coleridge's poem has seven parts and throughout, the rhythm gains momentum. We have a strong emotional response to the poem because we are almost literally swept up in its even, chant-like flow. The pattern is established in the repetition of lines having the same number of syllables, as well as by the steady use of accent in the same way. And this leads us to our first major consideration.

ACCENT: All poetry is written in some particular *meter*; that is, poems are made from a collection of lines which have a certain number of syllables, some of which are *accented* (receive stress) and some of which are not (receive no stress). We *scan* a line of poetry when we mark over each word whether or not it should be accented: a slanted dash (/) indicates that a syllable is to be stressed while one that is not to be stressed is marked ◡ . Thus, the following line of poetry, for example, scans like this:

$$\text{How vainly men themselves amaze}$$
(◡ / ◡ / ◡ / ◡ /)

Or again,

$$\text{The sword, the banner, and the field.}$$
(◡ / ◡ / ◡ / ◡ /)

The meter of a line is usually repeated.

$$\text{How vainly men themselves amaze}$$
(◡ / ◡ / ◡ / ◡ /)
$$\text{To win the palm, the oak, or bays;}$$
(◡ / ◡ / ◡ / ◡ /)

And their uncessant labors see

Crown'd from some single herb or tree,

Whose short and narrow verged shade

Does prudently their toils upraid; (Marvell)

POETIC FEET: Most readers will have noticed that the line seems to be divided into a number of repeated units combining the same number of accented and unaccented syllables. This unit is known as a *poetic foot;* each line of poetry therefore has a certain number of *poetic feet.* As the pattern of one foot is repeated or varied in the next, a pattern for the entire line and then for the poem is established. Feet containing different numbers of syllables, accented and unaccented, have different names. The following are the most common.

A.   IAMBIC: The *iambic foot* (an *iamb*) is composed of one unstressed syllable followed by one stressed syllable. The line we have looked at, for example, has four *iambic feet*:

How vain | ly men | them selves | a maze

This line has five *iambic feet*:

The God | dess with | a dis | con ten | ted air

B.   TROCHAIC: The *trochaic foot* (a *trochee*) is the reverse of an iambic foot. The trochaic foot, in other words, is made up of two syllables, the first one stressed and the second one unstressed. The following line has four *trochaic feet*:

Cast him | out u | pon the | wa ters.

C.   DACTLYIC: Not all poetic feet have two syllables. The *dactylic foot* (a *dactyl*), for example, is composed of one stressed syllable followed by two unstressed syllables. The following line has two dactylic feet:

Car ry her | care ful ly

D. ANAPESTIC: The reverse of a dactylic foot is an *anapestic foot* (an *anapest*); in other words, it is composed of two unstressed syllables followed by one that is stressed. The following line has three *anapestic feet*:

There is no | thing as Big | as a Man.

E. SPONDAIC: A fifth kind of foot has two stressed and no unstressed syllables; the emphasis, in other words, is on one plane. This is called a *spondaic foot* (a *spondee*); the following line has two *spondaic feet*:

Jump, run, | hide, shout.

Most frequently, the spondaic foot occurs in isolation near the beginning of a line which has another metrical pattern. The following line, for example, begins with a spondee and is followed by four iambs:

Milton! | thou shouldst | be liv | ing at | this hour

A student might do well to memorize the following review chart:

KIND OF FOOT	SYLLABLES
A. iambic	1 unaccented followed by 1 accented
B. trochaic	1 accented followed by 1 unaccented (reverse of A)
C. dactylic	1 accented followed by 2 unaccented
D. anapestic	2 unaccented followed by 1 accented (reverse of C)
E. spondaic	2 accented

METRICAL LINES: We have been examining lines containing different numbers of poetic feet. The number of feet contained in any given line determines its name. A line having only one foot is referred to as *monometer* (*mono,* meaning *one,* plus meter). Similarly, a line of two feet is called *dimeter,* three feet, *trimeter.* A complete table follows:

NUMBER OF FEET IN LINE	NAME OF LINE
1	monometer
2	dimeter

3	trimeter
4	tetrameter
5	pentameter
6	hexameter
7	heptameter
8	octameter

Lines of over five feet, and lines of only one foot, it should be noted, are relatively rare. Lines of five feet are the most common.

COMPLETE DESCRIPTIONS OF POETIC LINES: When we know the names of the poetic feet and the names for lines having a certain number of feet, we can name a line properly, referring to both the kind of foot and the number of feet. To return to our opening line, for example, "How vainly men themselves amaze," we can see that it has four feet written in iambic measure; thus the line is written in *iambic tetrameter*. The line "The Goddess with a discontented air" has five feet in iambic measure and so is called a line of *iambic pentameter*. The line "There is nothing as Big as a Man" has three feet of anapestic measure so we call it a line of *anapestic trimeter*. Usually a whole poem will follow a general pattern; the Marvell poem, for example, is written in iambic tetrameter. Although there may be a variation of a line length or foot, as long as the general pattern is the repetition of the same kind of line or foot, we can name the pattern of the whole poem.

RISING AND FALLING METER: After identifying and naming the metrical elements of a poem, we can make more generalized statements about the way the rhythm works. When the unaccented syllables come first, for example, (as in iambic and anapestic feet), the verse is said to be written in *rising meter* as we are moving up toward the emphasis; conversely, when the stressed syllable is followed by the unstressed syllables (as in trochaic and dactylic feet), the verse is said to be written in a *falling meter,* as we are sliding back and away from the emphasis.

MASCULINE AND FEMININE ENDINGS: There are other concrete things which can be decided about the subtle variations in a poem's structure. For example, if a line ends with an extra, or additional, unaccented syllable, it is said to have a "soft" or *feminine ending*. If, on the other hand, the line ends on a hard, accented syllable, (not additional) it has a *masculine ending*.

THE CAESURA: The pause in a line is referred to as a *caesura* and is often best discovered by reading the poem aloud. The caesura in the following line is quite obviously after the word Milton:

> Milton! Thou shouldst be living at this hour.

It should be noted that not every line of poetry has a caesura and that it is not necessarily punctuated. The use of the caesura affects the rhythm of the poem; the pace can be changed by the frequency of the use of the caesura and the strength of the punctuation used.

END-STOPPED LINE; RUN-ON LINE: A further distinction must be made between a line of poetry which pauses most naturally at the end of a line, usually with a completed clause or with the ending of a sentence, and a line of poetry which *runs on* past the end of the line into the next one before pausing naturally. The former is an *end-stopped line* and the latter is a *run-on line*. This latter is also known as an *enjambement*. An example of an end-stopped line is the following: "Inland, within a hollow vale, I stood"; an example of enjambement would be, "I shrunk; for verily the barrier flood/Was like a lake." The thought, or unit of composition, after which we pause, ends only in the second line and not the first.

Keeping in mind the techniques of basic versification which we have discussed so far, there are two verse forms basic to English poetry which we should examine.

BLANK VERSE: Unrhymed iambic pentameter. The form was developed by the Italians and introduced into English literature during the Renaissance, first by Surrey in his translation of Virgil's *Aeneid*. Since there is no rhyme used, the units of thought form the stanzaic divisions. Through the use of techniques like enjambement, end-stopped lines, etc., the poet is able to write verse units without rhyme. The form became the standard mode of expression for dignified verse forms such as poetic drama and the epic, although it has been used for every kind of poetry. Shakespeare's plays and Milton's *Paradise*

Lost, as well as some twentieth-century poetry, are written in blank verse.

FREE VERSE: Poetry composed in lines which are free of the traditional patterns of rhyme and meter and whose rhythm is based, instead, on the stress resulting from the meaning of the line and its natural and punctuated pauses. Each line contains varying numbers and types of poetic feet; however, although the strict traditional patterns of versification are not followed, free verse can not be said to be formless. A pattern of rhythm is established within the poem, and the lines move away from, and back toward, this norm. Although the form has been most widely used by modern poets since the beginning of the Symbolist movement at the end of the nineteenth century, poetry of this type was written by the Hebrew psalmists, Goethe, Matthew Arnold and others.

RHYME

PERFECT RHYME AND HALF-RHYME: Once we have observed the metrical patterns of a poem we should discuss its rhyme. That is, we must record the patterns of repetition of sounds as they are heard in the poem. This is not usually a difficult task, although certain poems depend for effect on very complex rhyme schemes. *Perfect rhymes,* sometimes called *exact rhymes,* occur when the stressed vowels following differing consonant sounds are identical—slow and grow—and any following sounds are identical—fleet and street, buying and crying, bring and sing. The sound, not the spelling, determines whether or not the sounds are identical. *Half-rhyme* or *approximate rhyme* occurs when the final consonant sounds of rhyming words are identical. The stressed vowel sounds and any preceding consonant sounds differ.

The following lines from Keats' famous "Ode on a Grecian Urn" exhibit a pair of perfect rhymes and a pair of imperfect rhymes:

Thou still unravish'd bride of quietness,
   Thou foster-child of Silence and slow Time,
Sylvan historian, who canst thus express
   A flowery tale more sweetly than our rhyme:
The "ess" sound is identical in the first and third lines, while

the "ime" sound is identical in the second and fourth. The first and third lines are half-rhymes, since only the final consonant sounds are identical. The second and fourth lines are perfect rhymes; the stressed vowel sounds are identical and the following consonant sounds are both the same.

The first four lines of the second stanza of Keats' poem exhibit two pair of half-rhyme, or approximate rhyme:

> Heard melodies are sweet, but those un*heard*
> Are sweeter; therefore, ye soft pipes, play *on*:
> Not to the sensual ear, but, more en*dear'd,*
> Pipe to the spirit ditties of no *tone*:

We can see that "heard" and "dear'd" are not identical sounds; nor are "on" and "tone." The initial consonants, and the vowel sounds differ, but in each pair, the final consonant sound is identical. It is not irregular, incidentally, for a poet to combine perfect and imperfect rhymes. Sometimes the meaning calls for an effect best achieved by an imperfectly rhyming pair of sounds.

MASCULINE AND FEMININE RHYME: *Masculine rhyme* occurs when the final syllables of the rhyming words are stressed. After the difference in the initial consonants, the words are identical in sound—contort and purport. *Feminine rhyme* is the rhyming of stressed syllables followed by identical unstressed syllables—treasure and pleasure. The following excerpts from Matthew Arnold's "The Scholar-Gipsy" illustrate these two types—the first, the masculine rhyme, "inquired"-"desired," and the second, the feminine rhyme, "flowers"-"bowers."

> But once, years after, in the country lanes,
> Two scholars, whom at college erst he knew,
> Met him, and of his way of life *inquired*.
> Whereat he answered that the Gipsy crew,
> His mates, had arts to rule as they *desired*
> The workings of mens brains;
> . . .

> And leaning backwards in a pensive dream,
> And fostering in thy lap a heap of *flowers*
> Plucked in shy fields and distant wychwood *bowers,*
> And thine eyes resting on the moonlit stream:

INTERNAL RHYME: Most poems are written with *end-rhyme*. This means that the rhyming sounds are found at the ends of the lines, as in the above lines by Arnold. Sometimes we find *internal rhyme* where the rhyming words are found within the line, often a word in the middle of a line rhyming with the last word or sound in the line. The opening of Tennyson's poem, "Blow, Bugle, Blow," illustrates internal rhyme:

> The splendour *falls* on castle *walls*
> And snowy summits old in story:
> The long light *shakes* across the *lakes*
> And the wild cataract leaps in glory.

We should notice, through the example of "story" and "glory," that using internal rhyme does not in any way prevent a poet from using end rhyme as well.

This discussion of the elements of the rhythmic pattern in a poem leads us to our next consideration.

RHYME-SCHEME: When we want to describe the pattern of rhyme in a poem or a stanza, we label the first sound "a," the next "b," then "c," "d," etc. As the sound reappears, we use the same letter originally used to label that sound. Thus, the lines of the first Arnold excerpt (used in our discussion of masculine and feminine rhyme) would be labelled: lanes-a, knew-b, inquired-c, crew-b, desired-c, brains-a. We would then name the entire stanza in this way, and summarize the rhyme of the stanza by saying that the pattern of rhyme is *abcbca,* etc. This is known as the stanza's *rhyme-scheme*. We might also point out the masculine rhyme, the examples of end-rhyme, and enjambement. In other words, we could present our reader with a great deal of specific information about the poem's rhyme—not to mention all of the information we could offer about the metrical scheme of the poem.

ALLITERATION: Other kinds of rhyme should be mentioned briefly. For example, *initial-rhyme,* usually referred to as *alliteration*. Here the same sound starts several words. Consider the following lines from Swinburn's "Chorus from 'Atalanta' ":

> For winter's *r*ains and *r*uins are over,
> And all the *s*eason of *s*nows and *s*ins;
> The *d*ay *d*ividing *l*over and *l*over,
> The *l*ight that *l*oses, the night that wins.

These lines are heavily alliterated. In the first line we have a repetition of the "r" sound, in the second line the "s" sound, in the third line both the "d" and the "l" sounds, and in the fourth line the "l" sound once again. Alliteration should always be noticed when surveying a poem in preparation for analysis. One should here search for possible explanations of why Swinburne chose to employ alliteration. What effect does the series of "s" sounds produce?

ASSONANCE AND CONSONANCE: Other words exhibit *assonance* and *consonance*. Assonance is the use of identical vowel sounds surrounded by different kinds of consonant sounds in words in close proximity to each other. There is assonance, for example, between the words "bird" and "thirst" because the "er" sound is identical in both words while at the same time enclosed by different consonant sounds. Consonance is, as might be expected, the reverse of assonance. Thus in consonance, consonant sounds are the same but there are different vowel sounds. The words "wood" and "weed" have identical consonant sounds but different vowel sounds and thus they are consonant.

ONOMATOPOEIA: Finally, there is *onomatopoeia*. This is the technique of using a word whose sound suggests its meaning. "Buzz," "crackle," and "hum" are often cited as examples, but some onomatopoeia is less obvious—for example, "shiver" or "quake."

SOME EFFECTS OF RHYME: Rhyme, a technique basic to versification, has aesthetic value as it functions in a poem. Rhyme creates soothing, pleasurable effects in poetry. When we have already heard a sound before, it becomes particularly pleasing to hear it again; the second appearance of the sound is like an echo which sends us inquisitively back to its source. Furthermore, through stanzas, rhyme has an organizing function.

STANZAIC FORMS

STANZAS: Patterns of rhyme are organized into verse paragraphs, or blocks of lines. Stanzas are the major divisions made in a poem in a regular or consistent way. A stanza, in short, is a group of lines and therefore a recognizable unit in a poem; ordinarily, each stanza follows a particular rhyme scheme. Some of the more common stanzas follow:

A.   COUPLET: A couplet is a stanza composed of only two lines which usually rhyme. A couplet is, in other words, one line coupled to another. An *heroic couplet,* found frequently in English poetry, is a stanza composed of two rhyming lines of iambic pentameter; in the following lines, Dryden describes a contemporary by using two heroic couplets:

> A man so various, that he seem'd to be
> Not one, but all mankind's epitome:
> Stiff in opinions, always in the wrong;
> Was everything by starts, and nothing long.

B.   TRIPLET (OR TERCET): A triplet is a stanza composed of three lines, usually with one repeated rhyme, or a rhyme scheme of *aaa.* The following triplet is by Herrick:

> Whenas in silks my Julia goes
> Then, then (methinks) how sweetly flows
> That liquefaction of her clothes.

C.   QUATRAIN: A quatrain is a stanza composed of four lines, either rhyming or not rhyming. As with the heroic couplet, the heroic quatrain is written in alternating rhymes of iambic pentameter. But in general, a quatrain is any four-line stanza, as the following one by Marvell:

> My love is of a birth as rare
> As 'tis for object strange and high:
> It was begotten by despair
> Upon impossibility.

D.   SESTET: A sestet is a stanza composed of six lines. Specifically, a sestet is usually the second part of a sonnet. As all sonnets have fourteen lines, they are often divided into an octave (see) and a sestet. The most common rhyme-scheme of a sestet is *abcabc;* an example of a sestet can be seen in the last lines of Milton's sonnet, "When I Consider How My Light Is Spent":

> That murmur, soon replies, God doth not need
> Either man's work or his own gifts, who best
> Bear his mild yoke, they serve him best; his state
> Is kingly. Thousands at his bidding speed

And post o'er land and ocean without rest:
They also serve who only stand and wait.

E. RHYME ROYAL: A rhyme royal is a stanza composed of
seven lines written in iambic pentameter and rhyming *ababbcc;*
Chaucer employed the rhyme royal stanza in writing *Troilus
and Criseyde*:

> In May that moder is of monthes glade,
> That fresshe flowres blewe and white and rede
> Been quike again, that winter ded made,
> And full of baume is fleting every mede,
> Whan Phebus dooth his brighte bemes sprede
> Right in the White Bole, it so bitidde,
> As I shal singe, on Mayes day the thridde.

F. OCTAVE: An octave is a stanza composed of eight lines;
specifically, an octave is the name given to the first eight
lines of a sonnet, the last six being a sestet (see).

G. SONNET: The sonnet is a fourteen-line poem written in
iambic pentameter. The *Italian (Petrarchan)* sonnet is divided
into an octave and a sestet; the octave rhymes *abba, abba;* the
sestet, *cde, cde,* or variations thereof. The sestet may also
rhyme *cd, cd, cd.* The *English (Shakespearian)* sonnet is
usually written in three quatrains and a couplet, rhyming *abab,
cdcd, efef, gg.* The sonnet form is an excellent example of the
close interrelationship of form and content—the development
of the thought in a sonnet is usually structured in terms of
the pattern of the rhyme scheme. The Italian sonnet often
develops a single idea in the octave—the linked rhyme scheme
supports this development—and offers a specific example in
the sestet. The English sonnet may present three arguments
concerned with its theme in the three quatrains—their rhyme
scheme allows this independent treatment, each quatrain
rhymes internally—and draw a conclusion in the couplet.

H. SPENSERIAN STANZA: One of the most famous kinds of
stanza is that designed and employed by Spenser; it is composed
of nine lines, the first eight of which are written in iambic
pentameter while the last or ninth line is written in iambic
hexameter. The final line, in other words, has one extra foot.
The stanza rhymes *ababbcbcc.* Although originally used only

HOW TO ANALYZE POETRY

by Spenser (in his *Faerie Queene*), the Spenserian stanza has
found wide usage by other poets, notably Burns, Shelley,
and Keats. The following Spenserian stanza is from Shelley's
The Revolt of Islam:

> I could not choose but gaze; a fascination
>> Dwelt in that moon, and sky, and clouds, which drew
> My fancy thither, and in expectation
>> Of what I know not, I remained:—the hue
>> Of the white moon, amid that heaven so blue,
> Suddenly stained with shadow did appear;
>> A speck, a cloud, a shape, approaching grew,
> Like a great ship in the sun's sinking sphere
> Beheld afar at sea, and swift it came anear.

I. OTTAVA RIMA: Ottava rima is a stanza composed of eight
lines rhyming *abababcc* and written in iambic pentameter. Like
the Spenserian stanza, then, ottava rima is a particular, special-
ized stanzaic form; it has been used by a large number of poets
including Milton, Keats, and Shakespeare; the following ottava
rima stanza is from Byron's *Don Juan*:

> But words are things, and a small drop of ink
>> Falling like dew, upon a thought, produces
> That which makes thousands, perhaps millions, think;
>> 'Tis strange, the shortest letter which man uses
> Instead of speech, may form a lasting link
>> Of ages; to what straits old Time reduces
> Frail man, when paper—even a rag like this,
>> Survives himself, his tomb, and all that's his!

Having familiarized ourselves with the basic art of versification,
we now turn to the tools with which we analyze the use of
words and the presentation of ideas in a poem.

TERMS FOR CRITICAL ANALYSIS

Samuel Johnson once advised his friends to "call a spade a spade." Nothing could be more essential in the analysis of poetry. The critic must be able to describe the properties of a poem just as a contractor might describe those of a house. He must examine a poem and be able to discuss all of the various concepts or techniques which its composition exhibits. In order to do this, one must have a sound knowledge of certain central terms used when discussing poetry; thus in this chapter, the most basic and necessary terms for critical analysis will be listed and described (in alphabetical order). It is hoped that the student who wants to analyze poetry will use this list as a small dictionary or handbook of literary terms.

ABSTRACT: related to the term abstraction, which is the process of selecting certain qualities out of many. In the process of abstraction, we choose various specific qualities to represent one large concept. Ideas in poetry are presented in terms of these specific qualities, representing the larger concepts. They are sometimes almost like suggestions of ideas rather than ideas themselves. The abstract is also the opposite of the concrete—the conceptual. And often the writer will take something concrete and transform it into something abstract, the purpose being to make something more beautiful, mysterious, or, ironically, clearer.

ALLEGORY: a prolonged metaphor. An allegory is a literary statement presenting its meaning in a veiled way; the literal meaning is a metaphor for the "real" meaning. Allegory, in short, is simply one thing consistently being presented in the guise of something else. In allegory there is usually a series of actions which are in fact symbolic of other actions. In an allegorical poem, everything being said in fact about the characters, the action, etc., is really being said about what that character or action represents. In Dryden's long religious poem, *The Hind and the Panther,* each of the title animals represents a religion and the poem is really about religion, not about two animals; but the literal actions conveys the allegorical meaning. In a beast fable, a fox on the ground flatters a crow up in a tree with food in his mouth. The fox tells the crow that it has a lovely voice, that he would like to hear the crow sing; the crow believes the fox's praise and begins to sing; in so doing, the crow drops the cheese— which the fox then eats. This fable is not simply a story about a fox and a crow; rather, it is an allegorical enactment of man succumbing to temptation and suffering the consequences. While pretending to be simply a tale about animals, it is really a moral statement on the human condition and on human frailty. The surface story represents another meaning.

ALLITERATION: the repetition of the same sound at the beginning of several words which are near one another. The most commonly known example of alliteration is the old jingle about Peter Piper picking a peck of pickled peppers. The string of "p" sounds gives a rhythmical, enchanting effect.

ALLUSION: the process of referring to figures or events in life or in literature, that are well known. Both this process of referring to another thing and the particular figure, event, etc., as named in the poem are called allusions. For example, if in a line of poetry we were to see the word *Job* we would call it a *biblical allusion;* we could also refer to the poet's allusion to the *Bible.* Allusion, in other words, is another word for reference. Many poets refer to other poets and to their poems and these are always cases of allusion. It should be noted that not all literary allusions are obvious; indeed, there are many *hidden allusions* and sometimes one of the analyst's biggest puzzles is trying to discover what an allusion refers to.

AMBIGUITY: the attempt to create mystery by suggesting several meanings and not making one more outstandingly correct than the others. A poet will say something in an *ambiguous* way in order to challenge the reader. The poet wants the reader to have some difficulty determining what is meant. By suggesting several meanings this process is inevitably magnified. This is *intentional ambiguity*. *Accidental ambiguity* often occurs, however. When the poet, through careless composition, neglects to qualify a line or an image sufficiently confusion or ambiguity results. This is of course to be criticized when discovered, just as intentional ambiguity is often praised. When a word can suggest several meanings it is an ambiguous word. Thus "puns" often are ambiguous references where various possible meanings are all perfectly clear. If one examines certain seventeenth-century poems one finds that the word "die" for example means *both* sexual union and death. It is often not clear precisely which meaning is correct—and we can never rule out the possibility that several will be correct. Thus ambiguity results when there are at least two different meanings which are possible or when meaning is very confused and completely uncertain.

ANTITHESIS: results when a pair or more of strongly contrasting terms are presented together. If words, ideas, or clauses are widely divergent but present together there is a certain amount of resulting tension which makes the line highly provocative. In Alexander Pope's description of Man we find the following:

> In doubt to deem himself a God, or Beast;
> In doubt his Mind or Body to prefer;
> Born but to die, and reas'ning but to err;
> Alike in ignorance, his reason such,
> Whether he thinks too little, or too much
> Sole judge of Truth, in endless Error hurl'd:
> The glory, jest, and riddle of the world!

We see many examples of antithesis as Pope yokes opposites together: God and Beast, Mind and Body, ignorance and reason, too little and too much, Truth and Error. Each line presents an example of antithesis and Pope is consciously working to produce an effect of tension caused by competing opposites; this tension, he is suggesting, expresses the essence of man who is, after all, a series of contradictions. In antithesis there is usually grammatical balance as well as contrast in meaning.

ARCHETYPE: the term used to describe an image that recurs throughout literature so frequently that it has become an established part of our mental vocabulary. The term grows out of the psychological theories of Carl Jung, but when used in literature it has the specific meaning of universal familiarity. An archetype is the original pattern from which are fashioned many representations of the same kind of thing. The scene of Adam and Eve in Paradise is *archetypal* because all other scenes in our culture depicting the loss of innocence are patterned on it. Christ is an archetype of all suffering men. The word derives from the Greek words "arche" and "typos," thus the "arch" type or pattern.

ATMOSPHERE: the general tone and mood of a work of art. An aesthetic atmosphere is created, for example, when the artist deliberately tries to evoke certain geographical associations in our minds. There is usually a group of words within a poem which collectively establish an atmosphere. If the poet used descriptions of large waves, churning sea, torrential rain, etc., he would obviously have created an atmosphere of storminess. Creating an atmosphere of love, or of hate, for example, can be an extremely challenging artistic problem. The term then describes the general "air" that we sense in the poem's setting.

BAROQUE: a style of composition which is extremely ornate. The term was originally used to describe seventeenth-century architecture—buildings strikingly ornate and embellished. This decor, however, is not accidental or even unordered. The ornate and the striking are usually made part of an observable pattern. Although not necessarily a weakness, in recent times baroque style is usually criticized. The student of poetry on the whole will not have particularly large recourse to the term but should understand it when encountered in reading literary criticism.

BATHOS: results when an attempt at creating pathos fails, and laughter rather than pity is created, or when the poet labors excessively to illustrate something which is so trivial that it is not worthy of his efforts. Pathos is the technique of successfully creating feelings of pity or sympathy; bathos, in contrast, results when the artist fails and we react not with pity but rather with laughter, boredom, and even disgust. The failure usually arises from the use of imagery which is elevated to a degree disproportionate to what is being described.

The resulting anticlimax creates bathos.

CACOPHONY: the appearance of widely differing and inharmonious sounds in close conjunction. There is a strikingly harsh combination of sounds and, as with ambiguity, it is often intentional. The poet uses cacophony to surprise or startle us, even to annoy us—but in any case, he will probably always get our attention.

CLICHE: a hackneyed or outworn expression or word. A phrase, word or idea becomes, through repeated use, very familiar and consequently less striking and interesting, even less meaningful; this is then called a cliche. A cliche is a stereotyped way of saying something. If a poet claims that his lady's beauty is like a rose, he is using a cliche. Or, if he refers to dying as "passing into heaven" he is using a cliche. Bad poets are most apt to resort to cliches when discussing universal emotions and events such as love and death. A supreme cliche yokes the ideas of love and death together when a poet claims that he is "dying of love." "Pining away," "smitten at first sight," "filled with undying hope," etc., are all cliches because they have all become merely conventional; they are no longer fresh and interesting; instead they are stale and unexciting.

CONNOTATION: one of the various implications or associations that a word carries. Most words have many connotations. If we say "home" for example, we are not simply naming a house, but rather an idea—having members of a family joined in one place. We may even think of apple pie and a large fireplace. A poet uses the connotations of a word to his own purposes and advantage. If he wants to direct the reader's attention in a particular direction he can do so by using a word that has the appropriate connotations. Some connotations are purely personal or subjective; that is, when I see a particular word I have certain *private* feelings and associations which you do not have; other connotations are *public,* that is, held by the majority of readers. If a poet says "she is like a daisy," we *all* respond to the idea of her fairness, freshness, radiance, etc. But had *I,* as a child, had a morbid fear of all flowers, I might make the further response of fear and disgust and consequently drive the conventional public connotations from my mind. No poet can of course know all of the private connotations; he deals primarily with public ones —and perhaps includes some of his personal private ones in the background. A word's *connotative meaning,* then, is extra-literal, that is, it exists apart from its literal meaning.

CONCEIT: a difficult, challenging, or highly provocative metaphor or simile. A conceit (originally from "concept") is a poet's attempt to posit a similarity between very different and unlikely things. A conceit is imaginative in an intellectual way; it is complicated in its conception but is therefore also brilliant and provocative. It relates one thing or idea to another intellectually. *Petrarchan conceits* (named after the Italian poet Petrarch) were unusual, original ways of express-ing one's various emotions of love. One might depict himself as a ship tossed in the storm of his loved one's displeasure. Dr. Johnson uses the term "conceit" to discuss the metaphysical poets of the seventeenth century. He had in mind the yoking together of highly disparate objects. Some find faults with conceits, particularly *metaphysical conceits*—those of an extremely complex and intellectual nature first used and made popular by John Donne and other seventeenth-century meta-physical poets. Some lines from John Donne's poem, "A Valediction: Forbidding Mourning," provides a good example:

> Our two souls therefore, which are one,
>> Though I must go, endure not yet
> A breach, but an expansion,
>> Like gold to airy thinness beat.

> If they be two, they are two so
>> As stiff twin compasses are two,
> Thy soul the fixt foot, makes no show
>> To move, but doth, if th'other do.

> And though in the center sit,
>> Yet when the other far doth roam,
> It leans and hearkens after it,
>> And grows erect as that comes home.

> Such wilt thou be to me who must,
>> Like th'other foot, obliquely run;
> Thy firmness makes my circle just,
>> And makes me end where I begun.

In this conceit Donne imagines that the souls of himself and his mistress are like the two legs of a drawing compass; when one moves in a certain way the other, though remaining stable, leans toward the leg that moves, and yet draws it back to the beginning. This is very imaginative and constitutes an intellectualized way of saying that he and his mistress are one—but not quite one. We see from "as" that Donne is using a simile to fashion this conceit.

CONCRETE: the opposite of abstract. It represents what is *real* rather than what is *ideal*. Concrete terms describe what actually exists. There is no process of modifying what exists; in short, what is concrete, *is*.

CONVENTIONAL: whatever is generally accepted or agreed upon. It is (a convention) a custom which has, over a long period of time, been given wide sanction. Thus in poetry we come across "literary conventions," that is, either instances of style or of content which are generally observable in all poetry. During certain periods, stylistic devices become literary conventions of the time; for example, it was a literary convention in the age of Dryden and Pope to write poetry in rhyming couplets. Many literary conventions are revitalized as they are used by other poets; other conventions, in contrast, become hackneyed and dull. The critic of poetry should be on the lookout for the use of literary conventions and decide whether their use is fresh or stale.

DENOTATION: the essential meaning of the word. As contrasted with *connotation*—the suggested or possible meanings of a word—denotation has reference only to what is conventionally understood by a word. The *denotative meaning* of a word is thus void of any emotional or subjective overtones. When examining any word, a critic should differentiate between its denotative and its connotative meanings.

DICTION: the use of words in poetry. When we ask about the diction of a poem we are inquiring into the stylistic and tonal qualities of the words which the poet has chosen. We are concerned with the vocabulary of the poem. A poet should always try to select the word which most appropriately conveys his intended meaning. Thus good diction begins with this process of selection. If we find a group of words in a poem which seem "out of place" or in absurd taste, then we refer usually to the "bad diction" of the poem. In discussing diction, then, we are much more interested in the selection of the words than in the exact ways in which these words are presented. Analyzing diction, in summary, is no more than examining the appropriateness of the vocabulary within a given poem.

DIDACTIC: designed to teach. It is of course possible to say that all poetry, after all, is designed to teach *something;* however, we reserve the expression "didactic poetry" to refer to that poetry which specifically wants to communicate moral or ethical instruction. We may talk about the *didactic elements* of a poem by observing the various words, phrases, and ideas which seem to be included only for an obvious purpose of moral persuasion. Poetry which urges us—frequently at great length—to improve our moral character, is considered didactic. Some critics have a strong distrust of the instructive cast of didactic poetry, arguing that poetry should please rather than teach. But the poetry of Sir Phillip Sidney serves as a constant reminder that it is possible to be both entertaining and instructive at the same time. But excessive didacticism usually detracts from artistic content and is thus rightly held in relatively low esteem.

DOCTRINAIRE: a poet or poem which is strongly influenced by *doctrines*. In other words, a poet is being doctrinaire if every poem he writes states the themes and nuances of his particular philosophy; if a Catholic were to write religious poems, for example, and each was simply an extension of Catholic theology, he might be said to be writing doctrinaire poetry. In order to refer to any poet or poem as doctrinaire, one must of course first explain the particular doctrines which are being expounded.

EPITHET: the phrase which is used to capture the most outstanding characteristic(s) about a person or object. If we call a man with red hair "carrot-top" we are using an epithet. In poety we judge the success of an epithet according to how appropriate it is for describing the particular subject in question.

Further, we must ask if the epithet calls forth the correct connotations. In the preceding example, we might decide that the top of a carrot after all is green! But in any case, any phrase which expresses a characteristic of a person or thing is an epithet—"Alfred the great," "Stonewall Jackson," etc.

EUPHEMISM: a figure of speech which veils the obvious word with another, less direct one. For example, if one says the sun "blossomed out of the horizon," one is saying euphemistically that the sun "rose." Usually euphemisms are employed to make some idea, concept, or action, more appealing—or, as the case may be, less unappealing—than it would be if stated directly. If someone "crosses into heaven" we shudder far less than if someone "drops dead." Euphemisms, it should be warned, are frequently suspect because the poet is forced into an over-reliance on artistic expression to mask something fundamentally disagreeable or even insulting (see periphrasis).

EUPHONY: the opposite of *cacophony*. In other words, euphony results when the poet has selected sounds which are compatible and harmonious. They create a soothing, melodious effect and are usually representative of good style. But as we noted earlier, cacophony can also be put to good use. Pleasing and sweet sounds have merely made euphony relatively more popular.

EXPLICATION: derived from the French phrase, "explication de texte," it means, accordingly, the analysis of a literary work. When we *explicate* a passage of poetry we examine its various components—imagery, ambiguity, rhythm, etc.—in order to elaborate on both intended and unintended meanings. An explication is a full account, a complete description of a poem or a passage of literature.

FIGURATIVE LANGUAGE: language which employs various *figures* of speech. Some examples are metaphor, simile, antithesis, hyperbole, and paradox. In general, figurative language is that kind of language which departs from the language employed in the traditional, literal ways of describing persons or objects. Using figurative language is making imaginative descriptions in fresh ways. It is usually immediately obvious whether a writer is using figurative or literal language.

FORESHADOWING: the method of giving hints in advance of what is to come later. Sometimes a poet will suggest—often through imagery—early in the poem what will happen later in the poem. This suggestion, similar to a movie "preview," is foreshadowing, sometimes called *adumbration*.

FORM: the organization of the parts of a poem into a whole. If a poem has fourteen lines it is said to have the form of a *sonnet*. In literature we usually discuss form as if we were picturing the total pattern, organization and effect of a poem. Form is the complete package which has a distinguishable *content*. In a poem we are usually able to describe the details of the form with the various tools of versification discussed in the preceding chapter. Some forms, recurring throughout literature, become *conventional forms*. The sonnet, the roundel, the hymn, the ode, the eulogy and the occasional poem are all established or conventional literary forms.

FRAME OF REFERENCE: the background of a poem. We consider a poem "in context" or "within a frame of reference." If we want to discuss a poem about a fairy princess we must know something about fairy-princess poems *in general*. If we are studying an Anglo-Saxon poem about monasteries, we must know something about other similar poems and about the conventional Anglo-Saxon attitudes toward monasteries. In other words, we must place the poem within the proper philosophical, thematic, or historical dimensions.

HYPERBOLE: a figure of speech which employs exaggeration. Hyperbole differs from exaggeration in that it is extreme or excessive. Sometimes it is used for comic purposes, but more often it is used seriously. Hyperbole can produce a very dramatic effect; Shakespeare uses hyperbole in a sonnet:

> In faith, I do not love thee with mine eyes,
> For they in thee a thousand errors note,

The idea of seeing a thousand errors is of course an exaggeration or *hyperbolic expression* of the poet's glimpses of his lady's imperfection.

IMAGERY: images, pictures, or sensory content, which we find in a poem. Images are fanciful or imaginative descriptions of people or objects stated in terms of our senses. When we discuss the imagery of a poem, we look at each of the images in particular and then try to arrive at some general understanding of what may or may not be a *pattern of imagery*. For example, we can refer to the pattern of disease imagery in *Hamlet,* to the imagery of light in the religious poetry of Vaughan, etc. When a pattern of imagery is found in various works by the same poet, or in various parts of a long poem or play, we can speak of *recurrent patterns of imagery*. Usually critics attempt to relate the various images to each other in order to arrive at a greater, less obvious (hidden) meaning in a poem. There is always a certain amount of mystery surrounding images because we can never articulate their precise meaning. When we study the imagery of a poem we are studying the entire world in which the meaning of the poem dwells. This is the world that the poet has carefully created through his decision to select certain words and images rather than others.

IRONY: results from the contrast between the actual meaning of a word or statement and the suggestion of another meaning. The intended implications are often actually a mockery of what is literally being stated. Sarcasm is a heavier-handed irony, usually harsh or biting, while irony can be light, comic, and playful. When a poet uses irony he is playing with the reader, asking him, as it were, to share in a private joke. The poet says one thing knowing very well that it will be read as if he were saying something else. This is delightful and refreshing because we are, for a brief moment, brought directly into the company of the poet. This effect is not limited to verbal irony. There can be irony in a situation, in organization, in a work as a whole, etc.; it is one of the most frequently recurring devices in poetry.

LYRICAL: referred originally to lyric poetry, that is, to poetry written to be sung to a lyre. However, the term "lyric" now designates a short poem which emphasizes the expression of the individual's feelings and emotions rather than external events or attitudes. When we speak of a line of poetry, or a whole poem, as being lyrical, we mean that it seems to express the personal feelings of the poet; it is as if he were singing by himself and we were allowed to overhear or eavesdrop. There are various forms of lyric such as the sonnet and the roundel, but in each case we witness strong feelings of self-expression. Although lyrical poems are no longer necessarily sung, they frequently retain their musical quality.

MEANING: though perhaps too obvious a term to be included here, is all-important in the analysis of poetry and all students would do well to ponder the word from time to time. When we talk about the meaning of a poem, we are talking primarily about the *significance* of its message. What, we ask, is the poet trying to *convey* to us? To what places—either physical or mental—is he directing our attention? The intended interpretations are all part of meaning. We must try to relate meaning to connotations; which did the author want to evoke, and which have we fished up from the pools of our private experience?

METAPHOR: the figure of speech which compares one thing to another directly. Usually a metaphor is created through the use of some form of the verb "to be." For instance, if we say, "life is a hungry animal," hungry animal has become a metaphor for life. If a poet writes, "my love is a bird, flying in all directions," the bird has become a metaphor of the poet's love. When the poet uses metaphor he transfers the qualities and associations of one object to another in order to make the latter more vivid in our mind. The metaphor in other words establishes an analogy between objects without actually saying that it *is* establishing this contrast. A *simile,* in contrast, calls attention to the comparison through the use of the word "like" or "as." If a poet writes, for example, "I was as happy as a lark," he is using a simile. He is making a comparison between his happiness and that of a lark; he is telling us, in so many words, that the best way for him to express his happiness is to compare it to that of a lark. While a metaphor directly suggests comparison of two things by creating an equation, a simile, in contrast, calls attention to the comparison through the use of the word "like" or "as." In summary, a simile says that one thing is "like" something else, while a metaphor states that something *is* something else. The comparisons made by metaphors are thus usually more subtle than those made by similes.

METONYMY: The substitution of a word closely associated with another word in place of that other word. If, for example, we speak of the government as the "White House," we are using metonymy. When a poet speaks consistently of a beloved, he is using metonymy.

MOOD: the creation of an atmosphere through the proliferation of certain common emotions. If everyone in a poem is sad or speaks of his sadness, for example, there is a mood of sadness dominating the atmosphere or world of the poem. Mood is thus the prevailing tone in a poem and this tone is established by the accumulation of a set of emotions. We can have a "gay" or "pensive" mood, or a mood of love. There is, in short, a mood for every set of generalized emotions.

MOTIF: a core experience around which an entire poem or work of literature can be developed. The motif, in other words, is the almost irreducible skeleton of the narration. Some conventional motifs would be the rape of a virgin, a young man killing himself after his love has died (throwing himself over a cliff would of course be even better), or a fairy princess riding off with a humble peasant (if he is ugly and she beautiful, again this is preferable; if he later turns into a handsome prince, well . . .). Motifs describe the basic centers of narrated action. The ones mentioned above are folk-lore motifs; a motif must not necessarily have this quality however. A motif, therefore, is very similar to a theme, which explains the basic center of meaning.

OBJECTIVE: impersonal, detached, and unprejudiced. When we make an objective appraisal of a work of art we are considering what is factual, devoid of personal interpretation. An objective treatment of a poem tries merely to deal with what is literal, implicit, or sometimes even obvious. In objectivity we find little emotion or personal distortion of the meaning.

OBJECTIVE CORRELATIVE: a popular phrase coined by T. S. Eliot. He meant it to apply to a description of a group of events, or a situation, which automatically arouses certain emotional responses in the reader. That is, there is no need for a personal intrusion by the poet because the mere things being described will *objectively* convey the meaning. It is a simple question of stimulus and response; when confronted with a certain set or group of objects or actions, a reader will immediatey respond in the only way possible; thus Eliot considered the objective correlative to be the main mode of artistic expression.

PARADOX: results when a poet presents a pair of ideas, words, images or attitudes which are, or appear to be, self-contradictory. However, while it may appear that these opposites are contradictory, paradox often underlines the possibility that both may be true. Paradox is employed in poetry primarily as a device of emphasis, of drawing attention to something. As with *cacophony*—incompatible sounds—paradox—incompatible ideas —shocks or jolts us to attention. Thus paradox, like cacophony, can produce dramatic and worthwhile effects.

PARALLELISM: a principle advocating that ideas of equal importance or significance should be treated at equal length within a poem. If, for example, one wrote a poem which was intended to survey the weaknesses of men and women, and yet only devoted one third as much space and thought to women as it did to men, then there would be a *lack of parallelism*. Parts of a work should be parallel with each other so that there is no extreme disproportion in emphasis. It would be as great a fault of course to devote equal thinking and space to concepts which were *not* equally important. If a poem was purportedly about a barn and yet the poet spent most of his time describing the farmer who owned the barn, there would again be a lack of parallelism; in short, parallelism requires equal treatment for equally important aspects of the matter under consideration.

PARODY: imitating the work of others in order to amuse. When one undertakes a parody, one tries to express humorously what some other writer either has expressed, or would express, seriously. In order to write a parody, a mockery of another author's style, language, and subject-matter, one must be fully knowledgeable with regard to the author being parodied. Unskillful parody is uninteresting and uninspired. Excellent and entertaining parody results when the writer has, in effect, done his homework—learned all of the details of the various nuances of another author's style. Like a caricature, a parody emphasizes the obvious characteristics for the sake of humor.

PATHOS: that aspect of certain poems which produces in the reader a response of pity and sorrow. We sometimes find a situation or character pathetic because there seems to be expressive —and sometimes unjustified—grief. This is different from the tragic sorrow we feel for certain characters in tragedies whose (see *bathos*).

n more spe-
cifically, the *voice* of the narrator or character in the poem. In
other words, when we read a poem we are listening to a voice,
but it may not necessarily be the real voice of the poet himself;
instead, the poet has put on a *mask*. This voice is *created* by
the poet and is not the voice *of* the poet. Often a young poet,
for example, has narrated a poem as if he were an old man (see
T. S. Eliot's *Gerontion,* for example).

PERSONIFICATION: the process of assigning human characteristics to nonhuman objects, abstractions or ideas. Attributing
personal form to such nonhuman objects and ideas is a standard
rhetorical device in poetry. Thus we frequently find poets ad-
dressing the moon as a lady, referring to *her* beauty. We talk
about the lady beauty and about old man river. In allegorical
dramas or poems certain characters are personifications of various qualities like virginity or virtue, evil or eternity, etc. The
poet thus *personifies* qualities or describes them as if they were
in fact people.

POETIC LICENSE: the poet's "license" or *privilege* to do something unorthodox in terms of diction, rhyme, or meter. That is,
under certain circumstances a poet may vary his rhyme suddenly without being thought to be a poor versifier; we give the
poet the benefit of doubt and assume that he could have main-
tained a regularity of meter but that he instead deliberately decided to introduce a variation in order to produce some special
effect. The poet, in other words, must be given some freedom
within the formal pattern which he has chosen; we would not
want the poet to be confined by his formal style. The effect
to be gained momentarily becomes more important than the
strict adherence to a formal pattern.

POINT OF VIEW: quite literally refers to the way in which the author views his subject; from what point is his view? From what angle is he observing his subject? All dimensions— temporal, spatial, philosophical, etc.—have vantage points. Is the poet regarding something that has happened or existed in the past, or rather something that still is to happen or exist in the future? Is he describing an event from the point of view of someone who was there or of someone who has heard about it? In other words, when we consider point of view we must ask as many questions as possible about the poet's attitude toward his material.

RITUAL: the form of conducting worship of one kind or another; also, any ceremonial and/or often repeated action. In ritualistic deeds of worship, bizarre things transpire. The entire action of the ritual is said to be ceremonial. We discover many poets treating ritual because it is, in effect, a poetic activity and thus subject to imaginative interpretation and description.

SARCASM: usually mean or vicious antagonism; it is not as clever as verbal irony. When one is sarcastic one is making an attack on someone or something. The method of this attack is usually to pretend to be making a compliment but, by the use of extremely sharp verbal irony, really to be making an insult. Sarcasm is the use of caustic or cruel remarks frequently presented by way of ironical statement.

SATIRE: The technique of holding human vices, follies, stupidities, etc., up for contempt, usually with an aim to reform. It is usually directed at ideas, institutions, or governments, rather than at individuals. The satirist is less inclined to spew forth personal dissatisfaction than ideological disagreement. The satirist tries to point out flaws through a humorous treatment. Jonathan Swift, incidentally, is considered the master satirist in the English language and a look at his humor and subjects will easily differentiate satire from sarcasm.

SENSIBILITY: a word which has undergone a series of changes in meaning. When used in connection with literature the word has nothing to do with whether or not something makes "sense" or is "sensible." It originally was a term used to describe the ability to respond emotionally to actions both good and bad; the eighteenth century considered this a virtue. It has since come to have a pejorative meaning—referring to all the bad qualities associated with sentimentalism. In current usage, sensibility is the name for the poet's sensitivity to sensory experience. T. S. Eliot made the phrase "dissociation of sensibility" popular in his essay on the Metaphysical poets. He used the phrase to refer to the unified sensibility, or union of thought and experience of which the sixteenth and seventeenth centuries were capable; now, in contrast, this sensibility was divided. A keen sensibility implies an ability to feel one's thoughts, and Eliot felt that this ability has been lost.

SIMILE: A simile is a direct comparison between things which are not particularly similar in their essence. A poet introduces a simile through a connecting word which signals that a comparison is being made; the most frequently used connectives are "like" and "as," but "than" is also used. If a poet writes, "she is lovelier than the ocean at dawn," he is announcing a comparison; he could also write, "she is like the ocean at dawn," or "she is as lovely as the ocean at dawn." In all three cases, the poet is presenting a simile which directs the reader's attention to a comparison which heightens the essence of the object or person in question; it is easier for us to sense the woman's loveliness through our sensing of the connotations of the loveliness of the ocean at dawn. If the poet draws a comparison without using an introductory connective such as "like," "as," or "than," he is probably writing a metaphor. (See *metaphor.*)

SUBJECTIVE: private, personal, emotional, or individual. When one reads any poem, one makes certain subjective responses to the poem. This is because every reader has a different experiential background. No two readers can share all of the same feelings about a poem; the ones they have but cannot share are all subjective. When the term subjective is used to describe a poem, we mean that the poem is filled with personal utterances. The poet is trying to explain his own private feelings and is giving a subjective picture of himself and his world.

SYNECDOCHE: a particular form of metaphor. The technique of synecdoche uses a part in order to signify the whole. Just as a caricaturist draws people in abbreviated terms, presenting a few characteristic and important parts, so does the poet sometimes choose to present only a small detail—but an important one—rather than a full description of something in its entirety. It is important to remember that only the *most* essential part be used to represent the whole—for example, "galloping *hooves*" represents "galloping horses."

THEME: is the central concept developed in a poem. It is the basic idea which the poet is trying to convey and which, accordingly, he allows to direct his imagery. Most of the images, in other words, are designed to present the central theme, or main idea, of the poem. The theme is, in another light, the poet's reason for writing the poem in the first place. It is usually an abstract concept which becomes concrete through the idiom and imagery.

FUNDAMENTAL APPROACHES

Now that we have reviewed the elements of basic versification and have compiled a list of critical terms, we are ready to consider the actual *approaches* to poetry that analysis requires. What will be our *method* of reacting to a poem? What kinds of poetry require what kinds of analysis? Where would we begin our analysis? How many different basic approaches to poetry are there from which we can choose? How do we select certain approaches? How do we combine them into a unified discussion of a poem? These and similar questions are the principle focus of this chapter. In short, we are concerned here with the fundamental approaches the critic can take when considering a poem for analysis. As might be expected, there are various pairs, or sets, of opposite approaches. Each of the approaches described is helpful in its own way and, ultimately, a complete explication of a poem requires that we approach it in various ways.

1. OBJECTIVE: The objective approach to a poem begins with a full *description* of the poem's physical or technical properties. The reader should try to elucidate the poet's methods and meaning in an entirely objective way. The critic should probably begin by presenting the most elementary information about the poem—its length, its rhyme scheme, etc.—and then proceed to more complex information. There should be a description of the basic versification of the poem; what kind of rhyme scheme does it have? How many feet are there in each line? What kind of language does the poet use—are there examples of alliteration, hyperbole, paradox, or any other rhetorical figures and, if so, why has the poet chosen to include them? How is the meaning of the poem conveyed through the use of these technical devices?

For example, let us suppose that we wanted to take an objective approach to Robert Frost's well-known poem, "Stopping By Woods On A Snowy Evening." The poem reads as follows:

> Whose woods these are I think I know.
> His house is in the village though;
> He will not see me stopping here
> To watch his woods fill up with snow.
>
> My little horse must think it queer
> To stop without a farmhouse near
> Between the woods and frozen lake
> The darkest evening of the year.
>
> He gives his harness bells a shake
> To ask if there is some mistake.
> The only other sound's the sweep
> Of easy wind and downy flake.
>
> The woods are lovely, dark and deep,
> But I have promises to keep,
> And miles to go before I sleep,
> And miles to go before I sleep.

We would begin our description of the poem by noting it is composed of four four-line stanzas, each with a rhyme pattern of *"aaba."* The metrical scheme is iambic tetrameter—there are four poetic feet in each line, each with two syllables, the second being stressed. Frost employs alliteration as seen in "*w*atch his *w*oods," "*s*ound's the *s*weep," and "*d*ark and *d*eep." The careful repetition of the last line is a major rhetorical device. The effect of this repetition is the establishment of the precise tone of what it means to have so many tiring miles ahead that must be journeyed before it will be possible to rest. We would probably offer a broad description of the physical action which passes in the poem—a man draws his horse-drawn sleigh to a halt in front of some dark woods to meditate on his journey through life. This would be an approximate summation of what has transpired. We must also analyze how the meaning of the poem—in terms of action and theme—is achieved by Frost's use of the technical devices we have described.

2. SUBJECTIVE: The subjective approach to a poem begins with personal interest in the poem. That is, when one has read a poem one has encountered the statement of a certain *experience*. Then one wants to respond to that experience through a consideration of one's own experience. In the Frost poem, for example, one might, for subjective reasons, conclude that the speaker is an old man who is tired or a young man who feels tired when he considers how many years there are remaining for him. A girl might, for subjective reasons, feel enough kinship to the speaker to decide it is a woman, rather than a man. Each of us would think of some of the possible "promises" the speaker has to "keep" according to what sort of obligations in life each of us might presently have. Each of us would make decisions as to the precise meaning of "miles"—for some readers they would stand only for seconds, as they might suspect that the poet was very aged and about to die any minute. For other readers, "miles" might be taken literally. Each of us would measure the narrator's intended journey according to different yardsticks.

In other words, a subjective response to a poem is molded by individual experience. When we are making personalized remarks about a poem—expressing our *feelings*—we are making no attempt to consider the poem's structure, harmony, or rhythm. We are concerned purely and exclusively with what the poem *means to us*. With the Frost poem, one reader might respond subjectively by saying that it is stupid: "why should a man riding a sleigh past a deserted wood be thinking about traveling thousands of miles?" Another reader, in contrast, might say— "yes, I have felt that way myself: sometimes, in solitude, it suddenly occurs to me that life is long and filled with many responsibilities; I have duties to myself, to society, and to God." Different readers would feel different duties. Individual conscience would determine individual interpretation and thus subjective response.

It would be wrong for a reader to take an exclusively subjective approach in analyzing a poem. It is not enough to base everything on one's private experience. One should say, rather, this is what the poem means to *me,* but I wonder how some other readers might interpret it. In other words, it is important that the critic of poetry try to imagine various possible subjective responses. In the objective approach there is little "wondering."

Every reader must of course ask basic questions in order to describe the physical composition of the poem. But in the subjective approach the work is significantly more difficult. For while it may be easy to articulate one's own feelings, it is very difficult to speculate about what others' might be.

3. GENERAL: As with the objective and subjective approaches to analysis, we have another pair of opposite approaches—the general and the particular. Using the general (or "universal") approach, we make various statements about a poem in a generalized way. That is, we might say of the Frost poem, this is another poem which shows man alone with himself contemplating his destiny. This would be a general observation about the narrator and the setting of the poem. We are concerned more with the fact that the speaker *is* alone than with *where* he is alone. We are interested in the *general world* of the poem. We view the poem as a representative situation in human nature; certain *universal* traits and attitudes of man are crystallized in the poem; we view it as a cameo of life. We direct our discussion to what general truths or feelings the poem reflects; the narrator is Everyman and the woods are the dark unknown. The journey he will take is the journey through life which lies before all of us.

4. PARTICULAR: The particular approach to a poem is of course the opposite of the general approach. The particular approach treats a poem as a special study of *something in particular*. In the generalized case of man alone, the particular person alone in this poem is a man driving a horse-drawn sleigh. He is stimulated to contemplate his destiny by a particular group of dark trees where there are no farmhouses. These particular woods are dark and set directly across from a lake; these particular woods are probably owned by someone that the narrator knows; it is late in the day when this man stops; he knows where he is. All of these statements are referring to the particular world of *this* poem. We are not interested now in its general relevance to similar worlds created in other poems; rather, our concern is with that which is *unique* in *this* poem.

The general (or universal) recurs continuously not only in poetry but in life. The particular occurs only once; it is unique, and thus, by definition, is never duplicated. The particular example of this man's stopping by these woods at this time of day is an isolated example of something larger which is universal—man's thoughtful solitude. The reader should always try to differentiate between what is general and what is particular in a poem. If we may refer to the content of a poem as *experience* (in contrast to referring to its form as *technique,* to borrow Schorer's useful distinction), what in that experience, we must ask, makes it unique? And, at the same time, we must ask, how does that experience suggest some universal pattern of experience?

It should be clear by now that no matter which approach the critic takes, his major task is asking questions. This is where every analysis of every poem should begin. Whether we are taking a purely objective approach to the poem's form and technique, or making a subjective response to the poem's recounted or distilled experience, we must always ask ourselves *what is, and why is it this way?*

5. POINT OF VIEW: We should never try to come to any decisions about any poem without asking the all-important question, from what point of view is it written? (See last chapter.) How can we describe the speaker's position with respect to his material? How can we describe the speaker? Does the poet tell us anything about the speaker in the poem through characterization? Does the poet purposely avoid informing us about the speaker? Most of our observations about the *persona* or *voice* in the poem will be based upon the attitudes and feelings expressed by the speaker. The point of view from which an experience is described is central to our understanding of that experience. We must state whether the poet is speaking in specific or general terms; we must explain his attitudes and feelings: is he bitter, gay, sad, happy, etc.? Does he seem to wish that the experience had never occurred? Is the poem narrated from the point of view of a detached observer or commentator—or from the point of view of someone who was there or was involved? In considering the point of view, then, we are basically outlining the poet's attitudes and physical relationship to the experience; at the same time, however, we must make some conclusions about the voice or persona of the poem.

In the Frost poem, for example, how would we decide whether or not Frost himself is speaking? One way might be to see if the same tonal qualities are discovered in the narrators of other Frost poems. In any case, we must always present our opinions about the narrator's point of view. With this in mind, let us examine briefly a well-known seventeenth- century song by Ben Jonson, "Come, My Celia, Let Us Prove":

> Come, my Celia, let us prove,
> While we can, the sports of love;
> Time will not be ours, forever,
> He, at length, our good will sever;
> Spend not then his gifts, in vain.
> Suns, that set, may rise again:
> But if, once, we lose this light,
> 'Tis with us perpetual night.
> Why should we defer our joys?
> Fame, and rumor are but toys.
> Cannot we delude the eyes
> Of a few poor household spies?
> Or his easier ears beguile,
> Thus removed by our wile?
> 'Tis no sin, love's fruit to steal,
> But the sweet thefts to reveal:
> To be taken, to be seen,
> These have crimes accounted been.

This song, found in the third act of Jonson's play *Volpone,* illustrates a point of view frequently discovered in both classical Latin and Elizabethan poetry: *carpe diem,* the Latin directive, meaning "seize the day." Here and elsewhere the carpe diem point of view is presented as the argument of an impatient lover. The speaker is urging his lady-love to enjoy the fruits now, to-day, rather than choose to wait until some later time. From beginning to end, the argument emphasizes the fact that the speaker and his lady should enjoy themselves, as he tells her, "while we can." The narrator is trying to convince his lady that there is no time like the present! It is patently obvious that Jonson's speaker is conventional and is modeled after the Latin poet Catullus. The same use of this conventional speaker is discovered in another seventeenth-century poem, Robert Herrick's "To the Virgins to Make Much of Time." The opening four lines read this way:

> Gather ye rose-buds while ye may,
>   Old Time is still a flying:
> And this same flower that smiles today,
>   Tomorrow will be dying.

The narrator's point of view is again "carpe diem." Thus in discussing point of view we must first determine precisely what that point of view *is,* and then decide whether it is more conventional than unique. In this way we are able to draw conclusions about both the poem *and* the poet's method of composition.

6. DOCTRINE: It is possible—and sometimes even necessary —to approach a poem philosophically. What doctrines does the poem illustrate? Does the poem have a doctrinal basis, or does it contain a statement of specific doctrines or parts of doctrines? To approach a poem doctrinally the reader must have a strong suspicion that the poet in question is likely to be associated with some set of beliefs or doctrines. Also, the reader must know the nature and subtleties of those beliefs and doctrines.

7. PSYCHOLOGICAL: In twentieth-century literary criticism it is particularly fashionable to discuss poems in psychological language. We often approach a poem as a study in human personality (with all its strengths and weaknesses). Often the psychological approach leads most directly to a substantial amplification of the meaning of a poem. Although we will discuss some of the complexities of psychological poetic analysis in greater detail in the Advanced Analysis section of this book, we can here mention some of the elementary or essential aspects that the approach involves.

To begin with, when we discuss psychology and its place in a poem we are primarily studying the poet's imagination. We are relating the material of the poem to the private musings of the poet. Is a theme, for example, the apparent result of some *dream* that the poet had? Is it an account of some particular way in which he views his own experience? Does it relate to his own growth as an individual? As all poetry is based on some kind of experience, and as all poets are human, we are necessarily caught up in the wide spectrum of emotional problems (caused by experience). We can and do speak about various psychological complexes; we might say, for example, that the narrator of a particular poem seems to have a *persecution complex* or is *paranoic*. We might say that a narrator loves his mother in an erotic or exclusive way and thus has an *oedipal* complex. There might be evidence of certain contradictory feelings which result in *ambivalence* in the poet's attitude. Of course no consideration of human personality and imagination can be complete. Even a psychiatrist would not attempt to learn everything about the workings of a particular mind. But our natural curiosity prompts us to consider such workings at least to the extent that they amplify the meaning of a poem. For example, a poem might present an artificial mood of happiness undermined by one or two details suggesting what is actually a serious or perhaps melancholic task on the part of the poet.

Not all recourse to psychology in the analysis of poetry is undertaken to arrive at an understanding of the poem; to a certain extent, we must be willing to use psychology to discuss probable responses to poems. For example, if we suspect that a poem will produce pity in the audience we are positing some sort of psychological relationship between subject matter and conventional response to that *kind* of subject matter. Furthermore, certain symbols call up various subconscious responses and are used accordingly by the poet in particular places in the poem; an apple will usually remind us of the Garden of Eden; a snake very often suggests temptation.

To what extent does a reader need to be familiar with the terminology of psychology before being able to make use of the psychological approach in analysis? Unfortunately there is no substitute for basic human understanding. If a reader *knows* what kind of feelings and attitudes a poet has, or knows why, as a reader, he responds to the poem in a particular way, and can explain this knowledge and reasoning in ordinary non-psychological terms, this is fine. If a reader happens to be familiar with the language of psychological analysis and prefers to put his discussion in such terms, this is also perfectly acceptable. The primary concern of the critic is to communicate his ideas and feelings about a poem, not to render that communication complex. To illustrate our point, let us examine briefly Robert Frost's poem, "The Road Not Taken."

Two roads diverged in a yellow wood,
And sorry I could not travel both
And be one traveler, long I stood
And looked down one as far as I could
To where it bent in the undergrowth;

Then took the other, as just as fair,
And having perhaps the better claim,
Because it was grassy and wanted wear;
Though as for that the passing there
Had worn them really about the same,

And both that morning equally lay
In leaves no step had trodden black.
Oh, I kept the first for another day!
Yet knowing how way leads on to way,
I doubted if I should ever come back.

I shall be telling this with a sigh
Somewhere ages and ages hence:
Two roads diverged in a wood, and I—
I took the one less traveled by,
And that has made all the difference.

On the one hand we could simply discuss the poem in a basic, philosophical way: briefly, a person can not travel in two directions at once. And given the propensity of human nature to continue in one direction, it is likely that once one begins to move—physically or spiritually—in a certain direction, one will probably not turn back. In this poem the speaker is reflecting on a certain time in his life when he found he had to choose to do one thing rather than another; he sees, in retrospect, that his choice was very influential on the rest of his life.

In contrast to remarks such as these, we could discuss the poem in a more specifically psychological manner. Our center of interest would be the poet's description of a past *decisional crisis*. Confronted with *competing alternatives* the narrator felt a certain amount of *anxiety*. Although he has made his decision he has spent much time contemplating it; it has been a continuing source of inner peace for him because he has convinced himself (*rationalized*) that he made the correct choice. In short, whether we talk about making the decision or about resolving a decisional crisis (*conflict*), we are talking about the same thing. As long as we can explain what we think the poet means, we are doing our job. In other words, we should be willing to discuss the patterns of human imagination and personality in reference both to the poet and to the audience, but we do not by any means need to be expert in our knowledge of psychoanalytical methods and idiom.

8. HISTORICAL: One of the most basic approaches used in the analysis of poetry is referred to as the historical method of literary criticism. This means that the critic interprets the poem within the history, or contemporary frame of reference, behind the poem. In other words, to discuss an Elizabethan sonnet, one must have a broad knowledge of the sonnet form, know something about how it evolved, and know how it was generally meant to be understood in Elizabethan times. The historical approach insists that a poem's meaning can *only* be understood within a historical setting. That is, those who use the historical approach do not allow for the possibility of making a *completely interpretive* reading of a poem. They would not acknowledge as legitimate analysis the subjective or psychological approaches, and would never base their conclusions on something as mutable as the meaning of imagery— unless they could understand the poem's imagery in historical terms. They would say, for example, "to the seventeenth century reader the word X would have meant Y because. . . ."

In other words, if one takes the historical approach one must be willing to do so to the basic exclusion of all other approaches. Or, at least, one must not use any of the other approaches until *after* the historical approach has been exhausted. This approach, then, assigns cardinal importance to what the contemporary readers *would have thought;* this response, in turn, becomes the basic clue to what the poet *must have meant*. While those using the historical approach admit that a poem can mean something different to the readers of a later century, they still maintain that the original meaning is the only *true* one, and that it can be discovered only through historical analysis.

9. FIGURATIVE LANGUAGE: One of the most basic and useful ways in which to approach a poem is to analyze its figurative language. That is, the critic concentrates his energy and attention on the images and metaphors and various other rhetorical figures which are found in a poem. Perhaps it is obvious that discussions of imagery and metaphor are the most popular; this is understandable, because this kind of examination is generally the most helpful in arriving at a general understanding of a poem. To analyze the various images in a poem is probably the greatest concern of all poetic analysis (except historical). For in the patterns of imagery seem to lie the darker and more secret meanings—both intentional and unintentional—which are to be discovered in a poem.

Almost every poem employs figurative language to some extent, but obviously some poets rely on it more than others. There are countless rhetorical figures such as paradox, hyperbole, and antithesis. But it cannot be too strongly emphasized that in using figurative language most poets are establishing analogies between people or things. And in these analogies lie the main presentation of the poet's ideas. To help us think about figurative language, let us briefly consider a well-known religious sonnet by John Donne, "Sonnet XIV":

> Batter my heart, three person'd God; for, you
> As yet but knock, breathe, shine, and seek to mend;
> That I may rise, and stand, o'rthrow me, and bend
> Your force, to break, blow, burn and make me new.
> I, like an usurpt town, to' another due,
> Labor to 'admit you, but Oh, to no end,
> Reason your viceroy in me, me should defend,
> But is captiv'd, and proves weak or untrue.
> Yet dearly 'I love you, and would be loved fain,
> But am betroth'd unto your enemy:
> Divorce me, untie, or break that knot again,
> Take me to you, imprison me, for I
> Except you'enthrall me, never shall be free,
> Nor ever chaste, except you ravish me.

We can observe the heavy reliance on figurative language in this poem. Donne refers to the divine trinity as a "three person'd God" and then turns Him into a kind of battering ram. This metaphor in itself is highly unconventional. Then the poet pictures himself as a town which has been captured by the enemy. He belongs to evil but desires to belong to good. The same idea is of course reiterated through the second metaphor in which Donne wants to be divorced by evil so that he will be free to marry God. He wants to be imprisoned by God on the one hand, and ravished by Him as if he were a young bride, on the other. Both the metaphor of captivity and that of marriage operate to underline the poet's basic attraction to divine things. Donne is literally begging to be adopted by God. The poet wants to be released from the shackles of evil, sin, and the devil in order to be wed, for once and for all, to the purity which God represents. We could explore the poem indefinitely; the point is only that by exploring the figurative language—and particularly the metaphorical bases—of a poem, we arrive quickly at the poem's central message. The metaphors, or figures, are what make the ideas alive or vibrant.

10. BIOGRAPHICAL: Closely allied to the historical approach is the biographical approach. In simple terms, we examine the poem in relation to what is known about the poet's life. Often a particular poem is subject to this kind of analysis simply by nature of the material. For example, in the following lines from Henry Vaughan's "The Retreat," the poet is discussing his desire to return to childhood:

> O how I long to travel back
> And tread again that ancient track!
> That I might once more reach that plain,
> Where first I left my glorious train,
> From whence th'enlightened spirit sees
> That shady City of Palm Trees;
> But (ah!) my soul with too much stay
> Is drunk, and staggers in the way.
> Some men a forward motion love,
> But I by backward steps would move,
> And when this dust falls to the urn
> In that state I came return.

It would be considerably easier to interpret this passage if we knew something of the life and particularly of the childhood of Henry Vaughan. There is of course a mixture here of sincere statement of personal conviction and of poetic statement of fanciful but less important desire. To understand thoroughly the poet's actual or final feelings about the desirability or enjoyability of childhood, we need to know something about his own childhood.

Emily Dickinson, as most people know, spent most of her life inside the privacy of her family home in Amherst, Massachusetts. She had a lonely and quiet childhood and life; her years were filled with many hours spent in utter isolation. This kind of information about the poetess' life helps us to understand her poetry; consider, for example, a short well-known poem of hers, "The Soul Selects Her Own Society":

> The soul selects her own society,
> Then shuts the door;
> On her divine majority,
> Obtrude no more.
>
> Unmoved, she notes the chariot's pausing
> At her low gate;
> Unmoved, an emperor is kneeling
> Upon her mat.
>
> I've known her from an ample nation
> Choose one;
> Then close the valves of her attention
> Like stone.

Our familiarity with Emily Dickinson's private world and with her lifelong tendency to reflect in poetry the self-chosen isolation of her soul, her inmost self, enables us to read this poem with a large degree of understanding. In other words, biography can often be of great use. But we must not assume that this is always true; if a particular poem seems to have absolutely no personal element behind it, we will not understand it any better by knowing the biography of the poet; if a poem's statement is very clear, we may not wish to investigate the poet's biography. The hardest decision is deciding when to use and when to avoid the biographical implications.

11. COMPARATIVE: Probably one of the most familiar tasks presented to students taking an examination in literature is to "make a comparison of the following two poems." This question is never designed to be superfluous, but instead assumes that through comparative analysis a reader will be forced to understand the individual poems more fully. We always appreciate beauty more when we place it beside ugliness; more importantly, however, we also appreciate beauty when it is compared with beauty of a *different kind*. Comparative analysis of poetry is extremely helpful. By searching for the similarities or differences between poems, we *are* searching. We are forced to consider the various aspects and dimensions of a particular poem. We can say nothing about how one poem compares with another until we have made an exhaustive study of both. In other words, making analytical comparisons of poems is a very difficult task, but one in which the rewards are usually equal to the labor.

When comparing any poems, one can easily begin by examining the different technical compositions which they exhibit. Maybe one poem will be written in iambic tetrameter and another in trochaic hexameter (although this last might make one shudder). Once the "groundwork" has been done, that is, once one has covered all of the simple and technical "facts"—meter, rhyme, style, use of figurative language, etc.—one should try to determine the nearest exact meaning of each poem and decide whether or not they are, finally, the same. Often two poems will appear to be about the same subject and thus one might prematurely conclude that they were "similar" poems; however, more often than not, one will discover, on closer scrutiny, that each of the two poets is describing the same thing for a *different reason*. In other words, we must search for the *emphasis* in each poem. What is each poet's primary concern? In short, we are forced to come to conclusions about the ends and means of each poet—asking the question we introduced previously— *what is, and why is it this way?* Whether or not the poems finally are similar or different is unimportant, compared to the actual analysis one has presented to make that conclusion.

Discovering a poem's intended emphasis is not always an easy task. Often we must spend considerable time trying to determine the relationship between the action (what happens) and the theme (what is meant). Once this relationship has been considered, and the reader feels confident that he understands the final meaning the poet is attempting to communicate, the reader should make a further study of the symbolism and patterns of imagery in the two poems. In short, in making a comparison between two poems, one should apply as many of the other methods of analysis as one can to each of the poems being compared. One can draw a line for two columns, place the name of each of the two poems at the top, and down the left-hand side of the columns label the grounds on which they may be compared. This is the easiest way to undertake comparative analysis; a brief schema will allow the reader to see whether his approach has consistency.

12. AESTHETIC VALUE: There are in English poetry certain works which do not have a great deal of meaning. We are not here concerned with those poems which accidentally are meaningless but rather with those which the author has purposely written *not* to stimulate us intellectually so much as aesthetically. The poet appeals to something outside our pure intellect—such as our senses, or perhaps our need for humor. Some poetry is very sensuous and whatever meaning it has is insignificant compared to the *effect* which the poem's words and language have upon us. Every reader is presumed to have some kind of aesthetic need; though generally indefinable, aesthetic need is combined from various personal appreciations for beautiful and, to some extent, sensually appealing objects, scenes, or descriptions. Each of us responds to certain descriptions in poetry in ways that we do not understand or even always try to understand. We realize that there should be some aesthetic value in poetry aside from whatever meaning is suggested. But some poems have an *enchanting effect* on the reader and we often enjoy sitting back in fanciful reverie with the poet. Consider briefly, for example, the following lines from E. E. Cummings' poem, "anyone lived in a pretty how town":

> anyone lived in a pretty how town
> (with up so floating many bells down)
> spring summer autumn winter
> he sang his didn't he danced his did.
>
> Women and men (both little and small)
> cared for anyone not at all
> they sowed their isn't they reaped their same
> sun moon stars rain

children guessed (but only a few
and down they forgot as up they grew
autumn winter spring summer)
that noone loved him more by more

when by now and and tree by leaf
she laughed his joy she cried his grief
bird by snow and stir by still
anyone's any was all to her

someones married their everyones
laughed their cryings and did their dance
(sleep wake hope and then) they
said their nevers they slept their dream . . .

While E. E. Cummings is talking about someone (i.e., anyone),
he is also experimenting with ways in which to produce various
effects on us. We respond to the strange couplings of sounds
and impossibilities, and wonder at the "stringing" of the seasons
or states of wakefulness. The poem's charm lies more in the
realm of aesthetic value than of thematic statement. There is
more mildness and lightness than heaviness and darkness. It
should be pointed out in passing that not all poems which
have aesthetic value are light and gay; many, on the contrary,
have a sombre or sometimes wintry cast about them. Consider
the aesthetic appeal in the following lines from Wallace
Stevens' "Peter Quince At The Clavier":

In the green water, clear and warm,
Susanna lay.
She searched
The touch of springs,
And found
Concealed imaginings.
She sighed
For so much melody.

Upon the bank she stood
In the cool
Of spent emotions.
She felt among the leaves,

The dew
Of old devotions.

These lines by Stevens, like those of E. E. Cummings, derive their greatest power from the effect they produce on us rather than from the intellectual guidelines which they establish. Stevens' setting is described in an aesthetically interesting way; we have a feeling for the character caught up in this place and this time; we have a kind of distant admiration for her. At the same time, she is somewhat unreal and generalized; we have no real idea of what she is like or of why she is where she is, sighing "for so much melody." In short, we find the poem enchanting without completely (or maybe even partially) understanding the poem's meaning. We can locate the source (or reasons) for our enchantment, but the poem does not exhort us to any particular set of actions. Our experience of the poem is sensual and general rather than concrete and specific. We can not even define the various abstracts; we merely respond to the experience of reading the poem in a pleasureful manner. And this is because the poem has a certain indefinable aesthetic value.

13. POEM IN RELATIONSHIP TO POEMS BY THE SAME POET:
A specific kind of comparative analysis deserves special mention. We often compare a particular poem with one or more poems by the same poet. We consider the poem in the light of what we know or can learn through study of the poet's other works. If we are not sure whether a poet is being sarcastic or serious, for example, we might survey his other poems and see if this poet is ever known to be sarcastic. Similarly, we can explain attitudes, themes, and sometimes images by way of associating them with their appearance in other poems by the same poet. In a way, then, this approach is similar to the *doctrinal approach* but is not limited to doctrines. If one poem by a particular poet can be amplified in any way by reference to other of his poems we should offer that reference. There is nothing wrong with considering a poem in isolation, as if the poet had written no other poems; but we can achieve a fuller understanding of the poem if we are familiar with other of his poems. We undertake this kind of analysis, in short, for the same reasons we undertake biographical or historical analysis; we are trying to fill in the "gaps" in our appreciation

of the poem; we are trying *not* to let ourselves be limited in any way.

For example, let us consider the following lines from Wordsworth's famous poem, "Tintern Abbey":

> To them I may have owed another gift,
> Of aspect more sublime; that blessed mood,
> In which the burthen of the mystery,
> In which the heavy and the weary weight
> Of all this unintelligible world,
> Is lightened:—that serene and blessed mood,
> In which the affections gently lead us on,—
> Until, the breath of this corporeal frame
> And even the motion of our human blood
> Almost suspended, we are laid asleep
> In body, and become a living soul:
> While with an eye made quiet by the power
> Of harmony, and the deep power of joy,
> We see into the life of things.

Now, if one had no familiarity with the rest of Wordsworth's poetry, it would be very difficult to analyze this passage. One would need to have some knowledge about Wordsworth's feelings about nature, and particularly about Wordsworth's mystical experiences as related in other poems, specifically in *The Prelude*. We would need a familiarity with various terms which Wordsworth uses in a special way throughout his poetry —sublime, mystery, mood, soul, harmony, joy, etc. We would need to understand his unique way of discussing what the closed eye "sees," in short, almost the entire spectrum or collection of images and words which together make up the "mix" in Wordsworth's poetry as a whole. In other words, knowledge of other poems by the same poet would allow us to understand a particular poem more fully.

14. MAN AND NATURE: Wordsworth's lines serve as an introduction to this and the next approach to poetry. When first reading a poem it is always useful to keep in mind two possible relationships, that between man and nature and that between man and society. By "nature" we mean the external, physical world; "nature" implies visible environment (in other words, we are not thinking about "human nature," instinct, etc.). A good many poems deal with one or both of these relationships; to a certain extent all literature addresses itself to them. For we are always thinking about man's relationship to the world of things and the world of people. How does man "fit" into the scheme of existence? How does he relate to the world around him? In the Wordsworth lines we sense that we are viewing man caught up in nature, man made one with the natural world and deriving obvious (if mystical) pleasure from that union. Any poem which is making a significant statement about man is likely to say something about man's relationship to nature. But this is not axiomatic; many poets overlook the relationship. The point is that the reader should always be searching for discussion of that relationship; analysis is improved by concentration on what is important and man's relationship to nature is important.

15. MAN AND SOCIETY: In this approach we are simply asking a question whenever we begin to analyze a poem, "is anything being said about man's relationship to society?" As with the reference to nature, we must constantly be searching for statements with reference to society. Not all poems are concerned with this relationship. But we must look for statements about Man and about a particular man. Most of us are familiar with all of the recent discussions of the "alienation" (from society) of modern man. On the other hand we speak of man's "involvement" in society. A man either is or is not included in the general world of people nearest him; he either is or is not known by the people or does or does not know *them*. Some poems seem to be designed to illustrate, primarily, man's relationship to society. Let us examine Edward Arlington Robinson's poem, "Richard Cory":

> Whenever Richard Cory went down town,
>   We people on the pavement looked at him:
> He was a gentleman from sole to crown,
>   Clean favored, and imperially slim.
>
> And he was always quietly arrayed,
>   And he was always human when he talked;
> But still he fluttered pulses when he said,
>   "Good-morning," and he glittered when he walked.

And he was rich—yes, richer than a king,
   And admirably schooled in every grace:
In fine, we thought that he was everything
   To make us wish that we were in his place.

So on we worked, and waited for the night,
   And went without the meat, and cursed the bread;
And Richard Cory, one calm summer night,
   Went home and put a bullet through his head.

This entire poem is making a statement about *a* man's relationship to his society. Nobody really knew what Richard Cory was thinking. They assumed that because he appeared perfect from the outside he must have been perfect on the inside; his suicide surprised everyone. Here is a man who goes into town (i.e., into his society) but does not really talk with anyone. He is a lonely man going his own way. Whether or not he is typical of Man is a decision each reader must make for himself.

16. THEMATIC: The last two kinds of analysis we have considered are both particular examples of thematic analysis. We are always trying to explain a poem's meaning in universal terms; we want to be able to talk not only about man's relationship to nature or society, but about his relationship to everything else as well—his family, love, hate, sorrow, deceit, hypocrisy, pride, birth, death. In other words, we are always trying to come to certain conclusions about the most significant part of a poem—its theme. What is this poem saying? Why does the poet have an optimistic or, as the case may be, a pessimistic view of human nature? What, according to this particular poet, is the human condition? Is man frail or weak? Is he courageous or cowardly? Is he proud or pompous? In short, in thematic analysis we are thinking in terms of themes which recur throughout all poetry in all languages. Man's view of himself lies at the heart of most poetry and every poet must suggest possible views, either directly or indirectly. Obviously, the indirect statement poses more of a problem. But let us remember that we are not simply trying to attach labels to poems; we are not quick to conclude that a certain poem is about man and nature. Rather we want to make such relationships play a part, large or small, in our overall discussion of the poem. We want to examine a poem from as many angles as possible, not perch somewhere and look from only one angle. Diversity of approach leads to the mitigation of bias.

17. EVALUATING: A final approach to analyzing poetry lies outside the realm of pure analysis. This is the evaluation we make of the poem. When we have looked at the poem in as many ways as possible, we should always make some kind of summarizing statement about the quality of the poem. Does it accomplish what the poet intended it to accomplish? Is it an effective poem? Is the quality of the poem comparable to that of other poems trying to do the same thing? How does the poem compare with other poems by the same poet? Is there any disproportion between the quality of the thought and the quality of the expression? These and all the other questions one can imagine should be answered by the final, evaluating statement.

When making this final appraisal of the "worth" of the poem, the critic must be careful not to spend too much time on a minor fault or too little time on a major one. The same rule applies to any discussion of assets. The critic's discussion should be fitted to the poem in every respect. And the best appraisal will come only after the best analysis; there is a necessary relationship between analysis and appraisal. There should be a combination of various approaches in the analysis of a poem, beginning probably with a brief account of the technical construction of the poem, moving gradually to an overall interpretive statement of its meaning, and a final statement of evaluation. If a reader does all of these things carefully he will be able to present a well-constructed overall analysis of any given poem. One is provided with a good many tools and should be able to do the job well. To analyze poetry is to ask questions—and then more questions. For almost every stage of analysis, every kind of approach, and every aspect of evaluation, is developed through answering the *right* questions. In the next chapter we will present case examples of analyzing poems; we will put our various tools to work, trying to understand the best ways of arranging them and combining them to achieve the best analysis of a poem possible.

CASE EXAMPLES

In this chapter we will analyze various poems. Our method will be to present a poem in its entirety and ask questions about it. In answering these questions we will be composing a critical analysis. The reader should here re-familiarize himself with the list of critical terms and also keep in mind the various approaches of analysis outlined in the preceding chapter.

CASE 1: EMILY DICKINSON'S "SUCCESS IS COUNTED SWEETEST"

> Success is counted sweetest
> By those who ne'er succeed.
> To comprehend a nectar
> Requires sorest need.
>
> Not one of all the purple host
> Who took the flag to-day
> Can tell the definition,
> So clear, of victory,
>
> As he, defeated, dying,
> On whose forbidden ear
> The distant strains of triumph
> Break, agonized and clear.

VERSIFICATION: To begin with, let us examine the versification of Emily Dickinson's poem. She has written three four-line stanzas (quatrains), all in iambic trimeter, with a frequent extra syllable in the first and third lines. The stanzaic rhyme scheme is *abcb*—in other words, only the second and fourth lines of each stanza rhyme, never the first and third (where the metrical variation usually occurs.

POINT OF VIEW: It is difficult to establish with certainty the point of view of the poem; the narrator could be either a man or a woman, young or old, etc. One thing is certain: the fact that the narrator feels sure that one who has not been victorious can best understand victory suggests emphatically that he (she) has been, as it were, on the losing side.

THEME: What is the poem's primary meaning? The poet's theme is summarized in the first two lines of the poem: success is considered most desirable by those who have never been successful. The rest of the poem develops the theme further; to appreciate the good taste of a sweet nectar, one must "need" —be hungry for it and unfamiliar with it. The second two stanzas describe the way in which the victorious soldiers (those who successfully take the flag) are unable to define success; those who have not been successful—those conquered—on the other hand, understand perfectly the nature of victory. It is particularly useful to observe that the poet introduces the word "definition" because we can consider the entire poem a successful definition of what it means to succeed.

THE READER'S RESPONSE: SUBJECTIVE INVOLVEMENT: One will respond to this poem subjectively in different ways. Those who have never known defeat or failure may not understand the poem at all; those who have never known victory or success will understand it very well. It is unnecessary to offer psychological discussion or historical analysis, because the poem is a relatively straight-forward definition of success. Because it accomplishes this one task well, we would probably evaluate it as a good poem. Its theme would not be clarified in any way by extensive analysis of the time when it was written; since its theme is universal, it exists independently of time. Similarly, its message pertains to all readers, not just to those who may be similar to the poet.

CASE 2: SHAKESPEARE'S SONNET 18

Shall I compare thee to a summer's day?
Thou are more lovely and more temperate:
Rough winds do shake the darling buds of May,
And summer's lease hath all too short a date:
Sometime too hot the eye of heaven shines,

And often is his gold complexion dimm'd;
And every fair from fair sometime declines,
By chance, or nature's changing course untrimm'd:
But thy eternal summer shall not fade,
Nor lose possession of that fair thou ow'st;
Nor shall Death brag thou wand'rest in his shade,
When in eternal lines to time thou grows't:
    So long as men can breathe or eyes can see,
    So long lives this, and this gives life to thee.

VERSIFICATION: As a Shakespearian sonnet, the poem has fourteen lines of iambic pentameter, and a rhyme scheme of *ababcdcdefefgg*. In other words, there are three stanzas of alternating rhyme followed by a rhyming couplet.

FIGURATIVE LANGUAGE: What use does Shakespeare make of figurative language? In the first place, the basis of the entire poem is an extended hyperbole. We remember that a hyperbole is a figure of speech employing extreme exaggeration; in this sonnet Shakespeare says his lady is more beautiful than a summer's day. The purpose of the poem is to develop this hyperbole with a certain amount of poetic validity. Thus, in the third line, Shakespeare immediately begins to point out the imperfections in a summer day. Sometimes there are rough and presumably therefore unpleasant winds; summer does not, after all, last forever, but instead gives way to the other seasons; sometimes a June day is ruined when the sun shines too brightly; and, finally, a summer's day is brought to a halt by night; darkness replaces beauty. In contrast, his lady is never dimmed; she never is lost to "shade" (which Shakespeare makes a kind of death). The main idea of the sonnet, then, is to prove that his lady has unfading immortal beauty; to demonstrate this the poet shows that the beauty of a summer's day, by comparison, simply can not compete with the beauty of his lady.

We should notice how Shakespeare uses figurative language in other ways. For example, we can point out the metaphor he uses for the sun: the hot eye of heaven. Summer has only a "lease," not permanence; summer, in other words, rents a certain amount of time during which she can be beautiful. The shade of night is a kind of Death since it destroys the brightness and beauty of a summer *day*. In other words, Shakespeare relies strongly on figurative language to convey his hyperbolic expression of his lady's beauty. The poet has chosen to begin by asking, "Shall I compare thee to a summer's day?" He then proceeds to this comparison, thus answering his own question in the affirmative. He carefully constructs a unified sonnet which argues cleverly and convincingly—and, more important, very poetically—that when compared to a summer day, his lady outshines and outlasts one by a great distance. His lady thus becomes superlative and the quintessence of all beauty.

The poem successfully answers its own question and does in fact present a good "comparison"; we can judge it very successful.

CASE 3: W. H. AUDEN'S "THE UNKNOWN CITIZEN"

(To JS/07/m/378 This Marble Monument Is Erected by the
    State)
He was found by the Bureau of Statistics to be
One against whom there was no official complaint,
And all the reports on his conduct agree
That, in the modern sense of an old-fashioned word, he was
    a saint,
For in everything he did he served the Greater Community.
Except for the War till the day he retired
He worked in a factory and never got fired,
But satisfied his employers, Fudge Motors, Inc.
Yet he wasn't a scab or odd in his views,
For his Union reports that he paid his dues,
(Our report on his Union shows it was sound)
And our Social Psychology workers found
That he was popular with his mates and liked a drink.
The Press are convinced that he bought a paper every day
And that his reactions to advertisements were normal in
    every way.
Policies taken out in his name prove that he was fully insured,
And his Health-card shows he was once in a hospital but left
    it cured.
Both Producers Research and High-Grade Living declare
He was fully sensible to the advantages of the Installment Plan

And had everything necessary to the Modern Man,
A phonograph, a radio, a car, and a frigidaire.
Our researchers into Public Opinion are content
That he held the proper opinions for the time of year;
When there was peace, he was for peace; when there was war,
      he went.
He was married and added five children to the population,
Which our Eugenist says was the right number for a parent
      of his generation,
And our teachers report that he never interfered with their
      education.
Was he free? Was he happy? The question is absurd:
Had anything been wrong, we should certainly have heard.

VERSIFICATION: Perhaps one of the most salient features
about the composition of Auden's poem is its irregular rhyme
scheme. Sometimes Auden uses alternating rhyme, as, for
example, in the first four lines; sometimes there are rhyming
couplets, as in lines 6 and 7, 9 and 10, 11 and 12; and sometimes there is a line whose rhyme is not repeated until five
lines later—as, for example, line 8, which does not rhyme
until line 13, framing the two rhymed couplets. The metrical
scheme of the poem is irregular; we can not say that the
poem is written in any one metrical pattern; we can not even
cite several different metrical patterns. For although the poem
has different pairs of rhymes, it is written as if it were prose;
each line is quite long and there are not pairs of equal length
except for some of the couplets.

THEME: What can we say in response to our previously introduced stock question, "what is, and why is it this way?"
Basically we have a poem which is not only irregular in its
composition but in its thematic development as well. Most
poems develop slowly; we begin somewhere and proceed
logically to someplace else. But in Auden's poem we are in the
same place from beginning to end: within a repeating definition
of Modern Man. No matter which detail of the poem we are
examining, the point to emerge is always the same: Modern
Man has, somehow, become very dull and extremely predictable.
He has the right number of children, he likes a drink, and
he owns "everything necessary to the Modern Man." The
poem is one large extended definition of a modern man. Each

detail adequately communicates the idea of the sterility of modern life. The last two lines of the poem introduce a different point of view. We have been assuming that the modern man being described is not particularly concerned with whether or not he is happy; but Auden asks us directly, as if he wanted us to be sure that the question of happiness is basically irrelevant. Modern man is more concerned with doing the "right" and the "appropriate" things; whether this mode of living leads to happiness is not really a consideration. Auden's answer to his own question seems to be logical: we can safely assume that the man being described was *not unhappy*—which of course is not the same thing as saying that he *was happy*. Auden has presented a poetic definition of a man caught up in the tight yet artificial fabric of his age. There is no room for moral speculation.

THE POET AS JUDGE: Is Auden making a judgement about Modern Man? Yes, it is safe to assume that Auden's mildly bitter tone conveys his boredom and loathing when he surveys the condition of Modern Man. Notice how Auden repeatedly emphasizes the man's normality; he was not "odd" in his views; his Union was "sound"; his reactions to advertisements were *"normal";* he held the *"proper"* opinions; he had the "right" number of children. The combined effect of all of these words— sound, normal, proper, right—is one of oppressive ordinariness. Because this man is ordinary he represents thousands of other "modern" men. Everyone else is ordinary. And this, Auden is arguing, is the tragedy of modern existence. We must remember—to take the historical approach for a moment—that this poem was written in 1940. The ideas of assembly production of automobiles, installment buying, etc., were being discussed critically for the first time. Concepts which seem somewhat stale to us now in the years of the twentieth century which are even further regimented were fresh and alive with horror to thinking people in 1940. At about that time America was entering into a new period of controlled living, of advertising, of mass marketing, etc. How easy it suddenly was to become ensnared in the web of modern regimentation.

POINT OF VIEW: What can we say about the "point of view" in Auden's poem? The tone of the poem is that of a mock-epitaph; that is, the poem, the mock-inscription on a tomb, describes the life of someone who is now dead. We are meant to reflect on the meaning of this man's life. The conclusion which is stated and restated is that there really was *no* meaning in this man's existence. And, the point being stressed, through tone, style, details selected for description, etc., is that we, like this man, are all leading lives which for the most part are without meaning.

FIGURATIVE LANGUAGE: Auden's poem relies very slightly on figurative language. He chooses to describe events and concepts in everyday, *ordinary* sentences. We realize that he is trying to produce a style which parallels the subject matter; how inappropriate it would be if Auden were to describe ordinary happenings in a bizarre or extraordinary method. Auden, we should point out then, is deliberately writing in a subdued, *plain style,* making little use of figures of speech.

For the most part Auden's poem seems to be very objective. Although we detect Auden's personal disapproval of the modern man, there is no overstatement; there is no strong personal or subjective statement. The poem is to be interpreted as an objective presentation of an extended definition of modern man. There is no subjective element, there is no use of figurative language; as a mock-epitaph the poem successfully accomplishes what it is meant to accomplish. In evaluating the poem we must ask whether or not the last two lines—so different from the style of the rest of the poem—are necessary. And to conclude that they are or are not involves making a certain subjective response of our own. To be completely analytical, we should try reading the poem as if it ended two lines sooner; if the poem does not seem to lose anything, probably the last two lines are expendable.

CASE 4: MILTON'S SONNET, "WHEN I CONSIDER HOW MY LIGHT IS SPENT"

When I consider how my light is spent,
    Ere half my days, in this dark world and wide,
    And that one talent which is death to hide,
    Lodg'd with me useless, though my soul more bent
To serve therewith my Maker, and present
    My true account, lest he returning chide;

> Doth God exact day labor, light denied,
> I fondly ask; But Patience to prevent
> That murmur, soon replies, God doth not need
>   Either man's work or his own gifts, who best
>   Bear his mild yoke, they serve him best; his state
> Is kingly. Thousands at his bidding speed
>   And post o'er land and ocean without rest:
>   They also serve who only stand and wait.

Before actually attempting to analyze this sonnet by Milton, the reader should reread the list of possible approaches of analysis. There are some which should be used and others which should be avoided.

VERSIFICATION: To begin with, it is always a good idea to present a brief description of the poem's form; that is, one should give the essential facts about the versification of the poem. Milton has written a sonnet and thus the poem has fourteen lines and is written in iambic pentameter. This is a Petrarchan, or Italian, sonnet. The second four lines of the octave mirror, in rhyme, the first four; while the sestet alternates *cdecde*. The overall rhyme scheme is thus *abba, abba, cdecde,* giving the poem a kind of tripartite structure.

DICTION: The diction of the poem is somewhat unusual. The mere use of the word "spent" for "used up" or "exhausted" strikes the modern reader as being somewhat odd. Notice also Milton's unusual way of coupling two adjectives with the modified noun in the phrase "this dark world and wide"; the normal procedure would be to place all of the adjectives before the noun "world," but Milton has, for effect (to emphasize the enormity of the world), postponed the positioning of the adjective "wide." Notice how each line usually carries one's attention directly into the following line.

THEME: As a sonnet, Milton's poem tries to establish one central point: to serve God one does not need to be actively working for Him, although some people choose to serve God in externally visible ways. Here it is useful to appeal to biography. Milton, before going blind, was active in ecclesiastical affairs and causes; he was known for his energy and physical vigor. When he became blind he felt the loss of the world of action; deprived of the ability to serve God in an active way, however, Milton realizes that through his personal convictions and faith he is still serving God. The poem has biographical significance since it reveals Milton's attitudes towards his blindness; biography helps us to interpret the poem because we know what kind of light (i.e., eyesight; or amount of light one can see) Milton now lacks; his life is outliving his ability to see.

RELATIONSHIP TO OTHER POEMS BY MILTON: This sonnet presents a case where one can better understand one of a poet's poems by being familiar with some of his others. For example, it is easier to understand any one of Milton's poems on his blindness if one has read all of them—and, in particular, his long drama on the blinded Samson, *Samson Agonistes*. The reader who wants to analyze this sonnet fully should read the rest of the Miltonic passages explaining blindness. Thus both biography and appeal to other poems by the same poet would be useful approaches to analyzing this poem.

It is probably obvious that when one is presented with a sonnet to be analyzed one should compare it with other sonnets —or at least one other sonnet—by a *different* poet. For example, it would be useful to compare the Milton sonnet with the Shakespeare sonnet, particularly with reference to basic versification and use of figurative language. Shakespeare's lines comparing his lady-love to a summer's day may seem unrelated to Milton's views on his blindness and his ability to serve God in another way than he had served Him previously; however, since both poems *are* sonnets, it is useful to compare them. We can better understand the distinct way in which each of the two poets uses the form to his best advantage; how, for example, might we explain the use of the two different rhyme schemes?

POINTS OF VIEW: Milton's sonnet contains both subjective and objective elements. From a subjective point of view there is of course the obvious revelation of his attitude toward blindness. More importantly, however, the objective point of view presents a new philosophical position of supporting God through quiet (or undemonstrable) inward action; the last line of Milton's sonnet—"They also serve who only stand

and wait"—has been often quoted in support of those who feel that it is better—or at least as useful—to serve God quietly through faith. The poem is a good presentation of this philosophical position although some would criticize the peculiar mixture of personal and objective viewpoints. There is perhaps some pathos and each reader must simply decide for himself whether Milton has successfully justified his position.

CASE 5: LORD BYRON'S "SHE WALKS IN BEAUTY"

I.

She walks in Beauty, like the night
 Of cloudless climes and starry skies;
And all that's best of dark and bright
 Meet in her aspect and her eyes:
Thus mellow'd to that tender light
 Which Heaven to gaudy day denies.

II.

One shade the more, one ray the less,
 Had half impair'd the nameless grace
Which waves in every raven tress,
 Or softly lightens o'er her face;
Where thoughts serenely sweet express
 How pure, how dear their dwelling-place.

III.

And on that cheek, and o'er that brow,
 So soft, so calm, yet eloquent,
The smiles that win, the tints that glow,
 But tell of days in goodness spent,
A mind at peace with all below,
 A heart whose love is innocent!

VERSIFICATION: Lord Byron (George Noel Gordon, 1788-1824) has written a fairly uncomplicated poem which reminds us of Shakespeare's sonnet which we examined in Case 2. Basically the poet is attempting to describe the beauty of his lady. In other words, the poet is writing the most conventional —yet not therefore necessarily dull—kind of poem possible. Like Shakespeare's sonnet, and like the majority of poems describing the beauty of a beloved person, Lord Byron's poem relies heavily on figurative language. The poem is composed of three six-line stanzas, each rhyming *ababab,* and each written in the basic metrical pattern of iambic tetrameter.

FIGURATIVE LANGUAGE: The opening stanza begins with a simile comparing the woman to a cloudless and starry night; from the simile we move to a series of hyperboles. The first continues the image of the beauty of night by noting the blend of the best darkness (night) and the best light (purity of starlight); their unique combination in her, figuratively speaking, make her more lovely by far than, say, gaudy day filled with ordinary sunlight. The image is striking because Byron is evoking a picture which is not at all conventional; many poets express the radiance of beauty through analogies to sunlit flowers and settings; few poets have expressed radiance through the contrast of starlight and the darkness of night.

The picture of his love is hyperbolic to the extent that she is seen as perfect; if she were just the least bit different she would lose most of her beauty; one tiny shade of light differing, she would only have been half as lovely (stanza II). The idea of the poem is of course ultimately to express the loveliness *within* the lady. Byron makes his point in the last stanza; the lady's loveliness reflects the goodness of her experience as well as her mind which is peaceful and her heart which is filled with innocent love. In other words, Byron ultimately wants to discuss personality, and pointedly shifts from a description of his love's outward appearance to a suggestion of the tremendous beauty which must be within her. Unlike the Auden poem we examined, Byron's poem has a visible development: a progression from physical to abstract beauty; a progression from concrete imagery to abstract suggestion of the images.

POINT OF VIEW: When we read a poem such as Byron's "She Walks In Beauty," we are not inclined to analyze it from a psychological point of view. Furthermore, we need make no appeal to biography or history. Rather we should point out that it is, after all, a conventional *kind* of poem—a poet describing a beautiful woman—and then continue by explaining the uniqueness (if there is any) of the particular poem. In other words, we say, "this is a conventional kind of poem, but notice how Byron imaginatively departs from convention by comparing his lady not simply to radiant light but rather to the resulting beauty when starlight and black night are found in conjunction." The idea of our analysis is to suggest the particular ways in which a poet develops an idea.

CREATION OF ATMOSPHERE: Byron's poem has what we described in the last chapter as "aesthetic appeal." There is a distinctly sensuous element in the poem; it appeals to our imagination and to our feeling for what is beautiful. The poem has a certain charm to it which defies definition. Part of the charm derives from the striking juxtaposition of the stars and the surrounding darkness. But part of the charm derives from the overall effect of the poem; there is the creation of a romantic atmosphere; words like "goodness" and "innocent" appeal almost unconsciously to our sense of what is lovely and morally worthwhile. The resulting *idea* of the lady is thus produced by means of various elements in the poem working in conjunction; the harmony of the poem blends with the harmony of the woman—which blends, mystically, with our own sense of harmony and its accompanying beauty. We are left not only with the sense of this woman's beauty but, further, with the sense that all is right with the world. There is an engulfing harmony; our aesthetic interest and instinct are stimulated. In short, there is a certain amount of *mystery* in the *world* of the poem. The lady's "aspect," as Byron phrases it, reflects the aspect of a world which is lovely and basically pure and good.

DIFFICULTIES OF EVALUATION: It is sometimes difficult to evaluate a poem like this one. The reason is that so much of its value lies in the aesthetic rather than the purely intellectual realm. We are inclined to talk less about theme and more about the suggested harmony. We are concerned not only with what *is* but also with what *can be;* the suggested inner harmony is seen as much in the light of something potential as in the light of something actual. The result of all of this vagueness is that any final evaluation of the poem turns necessarily upon subjective responses. We can describe the poem's meter and rhyme; we can explain some of the figures of speech; we can discuss the poem's movement from discussing outward to suggesting inward beauty; we can discuss the unconventional way in which Byron writes a conventional kind of poem. But we can not simply say, he is successful or he is not successful. Obviously, readers over the years have decided that Byron's poem is beautiful and provocative. No doubt a score of critics have pored over it religiously for hidden meanings. But the essential fact is merely that the poem is aesthetically satisfying. As with the E. E. Cummings poem, "anyone lived in a pretty how town," Byron's poem derives much of its beauty from indefinable sources. Most readers are content to leave some of the poem's magical beauty unexplained. We can never stress too much the possibility of "analyzing away" a source of loveliness. It is not a weakness in a critic to cease searching at *some* point.

CASE 6: JOHN CROWE RANSOM'S "HERE LIES A LADY"

Here lies a lady of beauty and high degree.
Of chills and fever she died, of fever and chills,
The delight of her husband, her aunts, an infant of three,
And of medicos marveling sweetly on her ills.

For either she burned, and her confident eyes would blaze,
And her fingers fly in a manner to puzzle their heads—
What was she making? Why, nothing; she sat in a maze
Of old scraps of laces, snipped into curious shreds—

Or this would pass, and the light of her fire decline
Till she lay discouraged and cold as a thin stalk white and
    blown,
And would not open her eyes, to kisses, to wine.
The sixth of these states was her last; the cold settled down.

Sweet ladies, long may ye bloom, and toughly I hope ye may
    thole,
But was she not lucky? In flowers and lace and mourning,
In love and great honor we bade God rest her soul
After six little spaces of chill, and six of burning.

A POEM OF AMBIGUITY: Byron's poem about a woman of beauty suggested this one; what kind of beautiful lady is John Crowe Ransom describing? Is his description very different from Byron's? Ransom's poem presents us with an opportunity to discuss *ambiguity*. There is a great deal in this poem that is not clear.

For example, it is almost impossible to determine precisely how the narrator feels towards the deceased woman. The opening reference to her "beauty and high degree" could be ironical. In the last stanza, when Ransom addresses other "sweet ladies," we can not be sure whether or not he is being facetious. Furthermore, we can not really tell just how the woman was treated by her husband; was she really the "delight of her husband"? The diction of the poem adds to the ambiguity. For example, the woman may have died partly from chills and fever and partly *from* "the delight of her husband." It all depends on precisely how we read the poem; where do we pause in reading the opening stanza? It seems as if Ransom repeats "chills and fever" as "fever and chills" to make a distinct connection to what follows, including the doctors marveling over her ills. Ransom, in other words, has deliberately opened the poem in an ambiguous way.

What does the poem tell us with certainty? We know that the woman who has died is fairly young because she has a three-year old infant; we know that she went through a final alternation of fever and chills and on the sixth exchange the coldness did not leave her, for she was dead. We know, from the second stanza, that she apparently went crazy. This is definitely implied when Ransom answers the question about what she was making, "nothing." We have only the picture of her sitting amid scraps that she cuts "into curious shreds." There is the suggestion (but *only* a suggestion) that these lace shreds are to become shrouds because she realizes she is dying and is therefore preparing for death. We can notice that in the last stanza when she is laid to rest she is again in "lace." We know that when she was having a spell she would not respond to kisses, wine, or anything.

THEME IN AMBIGUITY: But there is far more that we cannot know—at least that the poet does not want us to know. For example, how do we read the line describing the lady as "cold as a thin stalk white and blown," when we are later listening to the poet exhort other ladies to "bloom" for a long time, to "thole"—that is, to endure, to survive? There seems a certain incompatibility between the two parts of the poem. The poet, or speaker, is intentionally being ambiguous. He is forcing us to search for the true personality of the woman. Lord

Byron, in comparison, pointed directly to certain qualities of his lady and we could, without too much difficulty, arrive at the idea of her; in Ransom's poem, however, we can not ferret out that idea; the woman was young and she died of fever and chills and . . .? The question-mark is the clue to the fact of mystery. In the world of this poem we are somehow lost. The use of the word "little" in the last line of the poem somehow steals significance from her dying. And yet we can not clearly explain the theft.

Ransom heightens the ambiguity he has created when he asks, "But was she not lucky?" He implies that she was lucky because she was given a good funeral, was laid to rest "In love and great honor." Most people die without such recognition. Still, we cannot help but wonder just how lucky it is to go crazy and die at an early age of fever and chills. There is this paradox throughout the poem; and most of the mystery remains unresolved.

In four short stanzas—with unusually long lines—Ransom has managed to write what is, in effect, a mystery story. What do we make of the description of the doctors marveling "sweetly" about the nature of her sickness? Does this imply they cared more about the sickness than about the particular woman? If so, why? Why did the woman go crazy and sit alone wildly snipping lace into shreds? There is almost an infinite number of questions we will never really be able to answer.

THE READER'S RESPONSE: SUBJECTIVE INVOLVEMENT: Perhaps it is obvious that, in this case, we can not make use of most of the approaches of analysis we outlined in the preceding chapter. It is even difficult to make a subjective response to a world of mystery. We are not at all sure of how we are *supposed* to respond. The poet has concealed his exact feelings and the result seems to be that it becomes harder for us to define ours. We will make a certain subjective decision as to whether or not the lady truly was "lucky" to die. Some of us will base that decision on our reading of the ambiguously phrased opening stanza; some of us will base the decision on other factors—such as whether or not she was "lucky" because she died *when* she did, or *why* she did, or in the *way* that she did.

Our final feelings about the lady in the poem will thus arise in an almost inexplicable manner from the world of mystery which the poet has created and invited us to enter. There is no final evaluation that can be made in any exclusive way; we can judge the poem successful in establishing ambiguity (which often is appealing), but not in accomplishing what it was designed to accomplish, because we simply will never know for *sure* just what that was.

CASE 7: TENNYSON'S "MARIANA"

With blackest moss the flower-pots
   Were thickly crusted, one and all:
The rusted nails fell from the knots
   That held the pear to the gable-wall.
The broken sheds look'd sad and strange:
   Unlifted was the clinking latch;
   Weeded and worn the ancient thatch
Upon the lonely moated grange.
   She only said, 'My life is dreary,
      He cometh not,' she said;
   She said, 'I am aweary, aweary,
      I would that I were dead!'

Her tears fell with the dews of even;
   Her tears fell ere the dews were dried;
She could not look on the sweet heaven,
   Either at morn or eventide.
After the flitting of the bats,
   When thickest dark did trance the sky,
   She drew her casement-curtain by,
And glanced athwart the glooming flats.
   She only said, 'The night is dreary,
      He cometh not,' she said;
   She said, 'I am aweary, aweary,
      I would that I were dead!'

Upon the middle of the night,
   Waking she heard the night-fowl crow:
The cock sung out an hour ere light:

From the dark fen the oxen's low
Came to her: without hope of change,
    In sleep she seem'd to walk forlorn,
    Till cold winds woke the gray-eyed morn
About the lonely moated grange.
    She only said, 'The day is dreary,
        He cometh not,' she said;
    She said, 'I am aweary, aweary,
        I would that I were dead!'

About a stone-cast from the wall
    A sluice with blacken'd waters slept,
And o'er it many, round and small,
    The cluster'd marish-mosses crept.
Hard by a poplar shook alway,
    All silver-green with gnarled bark:
    For leagues no other tree did mark
The level waste, the rounding gray.
    She only said, 'My life is dreary,
        He cometh not,' she said;
    She said, 'I am aweary, aweary,
        I would that I were dead!'

And ever when the moon was low,
    And the shrill winds were up and away,
In the white curtain, to and fro,
    She saw the gusty shadows sway.
But when the moon was very low,
    And the wild winds bound within their cell,
    The shadow of the poplar fell
Upon her bed, across her brow.
    She only said, 'The night is dreary,
        He cometh not,' she said;
    She said, 'I am aweary, aweary,
        I would that I were dead!'

The sparrow's chirrup on the roof,
    The slow clock ticking, and the sound
Which to the wooing wind aloof
    The poplar made, did all confound
Her sense; but most she loathed the hour
    When the thick-moted sunbeam lay

Athwart the chambers, and the day
Was sloping toward his western bower.
Then, said she, 'I am very dreary,
   He will not come,' she said;
She wept, 'I am aweary, aweary,
   Oh God, that I were dead!'

VERSIFICATION: This somewhat lengthy poem by Alfred Lord Tennyson (1809-1892) can be analyzed in a variety of ways and we shall try to combine several of them. Perhaps we should begin by briefly noticing the versification of the poem. There is regular irregularity in the sense that Tennyson has chosen an unusual stanzaic form but once choosing has not varied it. Each stanza has twelve lines and divides naturally into eight lines of recitation and a four-line refrain which only contains short variations in meaning. The opening eight lines of each stanza rhyme *ababcddc* and are written in iambic tetrameter. The last four lines—or refrain—rhyme *efef,* and vary in length; the ninth line has nine syllables, the tenth has six, the eleventh has ten, and the last six again. Although the ninth and the eleventh are thus different we read them as if they were about the same as each other and as the preceding lines having only eight syllables. In short, then, Tennyson has structured his stanza in an odd way; this does not imply that it is cumbersome or unpleasant, but only that it is unusual. Tennyson has also arranged his lines of different length in a pattern of indentation; notice how the lines gradually move further in.

In thinking about versification we can note further the use of alliteration, the lyrical quality of the poem as a whole, the use of elision, the creation of atmosphere through onomatopoeia, the direct quotations within the refrain which enliven the heroine, the ornate imagery of flowers and creeping plants, the dominating end-rhyme, cases of enjambement (run-on lines), the dominance of masculine rhyme (said—dead, etc).

ATMOSPHERE: THE WORLD OF THE POEM: It is difficult to discuss the development within this poem. On the the one hand we begin and end with the woman Mariana wishing she were dead; in the beginning she is waiting for "him" to come; in the end she is waiting. The only difference is that in the beginning she has *some* optimism while in the end we sense that she knows not only that he has not yet come—but that he is never going to come. We do not know how old the woman is. Mariana, we sense, is rather aging; probably we feel this way because of the atmosphere established by the description of the aging vegetation—weeds and moss reflect time passing by. The woman is one with the weeds, the moss, the black crusts formed on the flower-pots. The world of the poem is one of extreme dreariness; the dominant dreary-aweary repeating rhyme in the refrain reminds us continuously that we are temporarily enfolded in a dark and lonely silent world.

We know that Mariana has not had many visitors recently; the clinking latch is "unlifted." Tennyson might even be suggesting that the woman has *never* had a visitor. There is a kind of indefinable eternal rotting occurring in the poem. That sounds indelicate but how else can we describe the background of the poem which is moving longingly toward *death* as a solution. "I would that I were dead," is a phrase being used not simply as a lyrical utterance; rather it is a statement of despair, a statement of utter isolation.

THEME: MAN AND SOCIETY: *Mariana* can be discussed in terms of man and society. We are examining a woman living in isolation, desperately waiting for some man, in a sense a representative of society, to come and enter her world. There is a kind of sheer horror in her wish to be *seen* as well as to see. She longs for union with society; it does not matter that the man Mariana awaits is probably someone whom she loves. Because above that he is also presumably coming *from* somewhere else. Through him she could make contact with society; through him she could escape her loneliness and alienation.

POINT OF VIEW: From a psychological point of view, *Mariana* can be read as a study in human aspiration; within the sagging walls of her "dreamy house" Mariana hopes that someone will come. And yet we sense that she knows he will never come; it is as if she knew she has no right even to hope, but that she nevertheless indulges herself. To be deprived of hope is to be deprived of life. In terms of human psychology, it is not as important that the visitor will never come, as it is that Mariana hopes he will come. Her often repeated death-wish is not a casual expression; it gives substance to the horror created by the probability that her visitor will never arrive. The various adjectives scattered throughout the poem—lonely, dreary, broken, glooming, gnarled, etc.—create a prevalent mood of lonely disaster. We, as readers, are peeking in on a kind of metaphysical loneliness which has the power to thrust an individual into an almost meaningless death. There is unrealistic hope and there is death. The combination of the two evokes a greater sense of horror than could either one alone. Psychologically the poem reflects what can be considered a universal situation: man alone in desperation and inclining toward death. The desperation and the accompanying inclination are not as incompatible as one might think.

Each of us will make a different subjective response to the poem. Tennyson himself is not being completely objective. We sense that the poet is familiar with loneliness and isolation, or at least that he has experienced the desolation of waiting for someone—presumably beloved—who never comes. The poem has a personal tone. On the other hand, the fact that the death-wish statement is always included in the refrain makes some readers suspect that the entire set of emotions is more or less artificial. Let us decide here and now that a refrain is not necessarily to be considered only in terms of form; the meaning of a refrain is equally important and certainly no less sincere because included in the form of a refrain. Most readers are familiar with refrain poems read to them as children and thus have decided that all refrain poems are "suspect." Tennyson's *Mariana,* a provocative and serious poem which makes use of a refrain, should be sufficient answer to that naive opinion.

IMAGERY: *Mariana* is a very delicate combination of colors, sounds, and other physical properties which all reflect the emotional outlook of the heroine. The *natural description* in the poem is carefully presented so as to produce the greatest effect on the reader. The picture of creeping "marish-mosses," or of rusty nails together with the strange sounds of the cock, the low of the oxen, etc., produce by themselves *and* collectively a strange world. The past is mysteriously present; there is a certain paradox in the fact that Mariana hears "old footsteps" trodding along upstairs, and sees "old faces." The various images translate into an almost *imaginary* world. Tennyson's ability to focus on the bizarre foundations of human aspiration and despair creates this world and its probable end in death.

CASE 8: ELINOR WYLIE'S "THE EAGLE AND THE MOLE"

Avoid the reeking herd,
Shun the polluted flock,
Live like that stoic bird,
The eagle of the rock.

The huddled warmth of crowds
Begets and foster hate;
He keeps, above the clouds,
His cliff inviolate.

When flocks are folded warm,
And herds to shelter run,
He sails above the storm,
He stares into the sun.

If in the eagle's track
Your sinews cannot leap,
Avoid the lathered pack,
Turn from the steaming sheep.

If you would keep your soul
From spotted sight or sound,
Live like the velvet mole;
Go burrow underground.

And there hold intercourse
With roots of trees and stones,
With rivers at their source,
And disembodied bones.

TITLE: Sometimes the best place to begin one's analysis of a poem is with the title. In Elinor Wylie's poem, we should thus ponder the title and ask why she has chosen to describe the eagle and the mole. What do these two seemingly very different creatures have in common? The answer of course constitutes the bulk of the poem: both are sufficiently removed from the crowds. The eagle flies high over the masses while the mole tunnels far below them. In both cases we see that the poet is admiring independence. The *means* of being independent is far less important than the independence itself: if you can not follow in the eagle's path, follow that of the mole. It makes no difference how you achieve independence as long as you do achieve it.

VERSIFICATION AND STRUCTURE: Written primarily in iambic trimeter, the poem is very tightly organized. Notice how each of the first five stanzas divides naturally into two sections, one describing the "reeking," "polluted" flock—the ugly, common masses living in hatred, etc.—and one describing the natural freedom and strength of the eagle or the mole. Notice how the various adjectives establish a sharp contrast between the gregarious flocks and the independent eagle and mole.

THEME: The poem is short and to the point. We have been able to arrive at an understanding of both meaning and composition merely by pondering the title in relation to the poem. Both the meaning—the necessity of personal freedom—and the organization follow logically from the basic duality presented in the title. In other words, if we find a short poem with a striking title, we can often most quickly analyze the poem sufficiently by explaining that title.

CASE 9: W. H. DAVIES' "LEISURE"

> What is this life, if, full of care,
> We have no time to stand and stare,
>
> No time to stand beneath the boughs
> And stare as long as sheep or cows.
>
> No time to see, when woods we pass,
> Where squirrels hide their nuts in grass.
>
> No time to see, in broad daylight,
> Streams full of stars, like skies at night.
>
> No time to turn at Beauty's glance,
> And watch her feet, how they can dance.

No time to wait till her mouth can
Enrich that smile her eyes began.

A poor life this if, full of care,
We have no time to stand and stare.

TITLE AND THEME: This poem again gives us an example for analysis through consideration of title. Leisure is being discussed in fairly concrete terms. The poet presents his basic philosophy in the opening of the poem—which after all is a request for the title word, "leisure." The poet is asking what kind of life this would be if we had no leisure time. The first and last stanzas make this central point, while the middle five stanzas describe some of the things we would miss if we did not have leisure, or "time to stand and stare." The poet chooses both detailed and broad pictures—both squirrel's places in the grass for storing nuts and sparkling streams. We would have not time in which we could study Beauty in all her fullness. Instead we could only catch glimpses; we could see bright eyes but not have enough time to see the smile that follows. This short and simple poem is content to repeat the same point over and over again—or simply make one point, as it were. By contemplating the title we must ask ourselves, what is the "leisure" that the poet is describing? What is his attitude toward leisure? Why does he consider leisure important? Why has the poet chosen to use a simple technical structure? The answer to the last is that the poet is talking about simple things, about the little beauties of life which we take for granted but which we would miss very much if we were suddenly to be deprived of our time "to stand and stare." Thus the poet has deliberately chosen to write in simple rhyming couplets of iambic tetrameter. The form is simple, the meaning is simple, and, perhaps most emphatically, the title is simple. Just one word, "leisure." The title again underlines both the meaning and the composition of the poem.

CASE 10:   HENRY VAUGHAN'S "THE WATER-FALL"

With what deep murmurs through time's silent stealth
Doth thy transparent, cool and wat'ry wealth
     Here flowing fall,
     And chide, and call,

As if his liquid, loose retinue staid
Ling'ring, and were of this steep place afraid,
    The common pass
    Where, clear as glass,
    All must descend
    Not to an end:
But quicken'd by this deep and rocky grave,
Rise to a longer course more bright and brave.

    Dear stream! dear bank, where often I
    Have sat, and pleas'd my pensive eye,
    Why, since each drop of thy quick store
    Runs thither, whence it flow'd before,
    Should poor souls fear a shade or night,
    Who came (sure) from a sea of light?
    Or since those drops are all sent back
    So sure to thee, that none doth lack,
    Why should frail fresh doubt any more
    That what God takes, he'll not restore?
    O useful element and clear!
    My sacred wash and cleanser here,
    My first consigner unto those
    Fountains of life, where the lamb goes,
    What sublime truths, and wholesome themes,
    Lodge in thy mystical, deep streams!
    Such as dull man can never find
    Unless that Spirit lead his mind,
    Which first upon thy face did move,
    And hatch'd all with his quick'ning love,
    As this loud brook's incessant fall
    In streaming rings restagnates all,
    Which reach by course the bank, and then
    Are no more seen, just so pass men.
    O my invisible estate,
    My glorious liberty, still late!
    Thou art the channel my soul seeks,
    Not this with cataracts and creeks.

VERSIFICATION: The versification of Vaughan's poem is unusual so we might as well begin our analysis there. The first
section of the poem is constructed of three rhyming couplets of
iambic pentameter, separated by several couplets of iambic

dimeter. The mixture of short and long lines is probably at least remotely suggestive of the movement of a waterfall, the long lines representing the steep plunge of the water over a cliff. If not visual, the alternation of short and long couplets offers the reader a rhythmic effect which again suggests the rhythmic evenness of a cascading waterfall. From another point of view the second section of the poem could be seen as the longer part of a waterfall. Written in unbroken, unvarying couplets of iambic tetrameter, the lines flow evenly in a long column. In meter and in rhythm the poem is definitely filled with the suggestiveness of flowing water.

THEME: MAN AND NATURE: Thinking through our list of various approaches of analysis, we realize that Vaughan's poem has *something* to do with the relationship between man and nature. It is at first difficult to decide precisely what that relationship is. The voice in the poem sees in the waterfall the continuity of life. The water now flows in one direction; later it will flow in another. Water is constantly flowing in all directions on the earth and reminds the poet that we will all eventually flow back to God, just as surely as we have flowed *from* Him in the past. What God takes away at one point, He will restore at another. The poet is finding God's presence in nature; he is not making nature God. The distinction is between a blend of Christian mysticism, and pantheism. The waterfall carries water through time, just as life itself moves people through time. The waterfall offers the poet the opportunity to create an analogy which will illuminate his relationship to God. The water goes tumbling over the waterfall "not to an end"; that is, although the water crashes down violently as if it were being destroyed, in fact, it has not gone into a grave permanently but instead from this grave will "rise to a longer course more bright and brave." The analogy is that man does not come to an end when he dies, but rather then begins his journey toward God. Why should we be afraid of death or darkness when we will inevitably conclude by returning to the world of light from whence we originally came? Just as the circles created by the falling water in the brook become invisible when they reach the bank, so does man finally pass into invisibility —where his ultimate liberty is located. The poet is confident that he will be returned to God's heavenly care and the world of light.

The poem makes a statement primarily about man and his destiny. But the mere fact that the analogy is drawn from a natural landscape means that something is being said about man and nature. The idea being presented is that man can discover in nature some of the religious mysteries which he knows to exist in his relationship to a deity. In the world of nature, in other words, man can search for religious meaning. There are clues, parallels, analogies, etc., to be found in nature. If the poet wants to increase his self-knowledge as well as his understanding of his destiny, let him wander into the natural world with the detective's eye. Vaughan makes the poem an expression of this potentiality of man in nature when he writes, "What sublime truths, and wholesome themes,/ Lodge in thy mystical, deep streams!" In other words, the poet knows that there are certain truths which can be discovered through an analysis of the natural landscape. Analyzing the suggestiveness of the waterfall is actually analyzing the suggestiveness of all of nature. The poem thus has a double representation —of man's ultimate religious destiny on the one hand, and of man's ability to learn about that destiny through the examination of the surrounding physical world.

THE HISTORICAL APPROACH: If we were to understand the poem as Vaughan and his contemporaries understood it, we would need to understand something of the theory of "correspondence" in which Vaughan and many others believed. This theory held that natural objects corresponded to celestial objects, and that things on this earth are suggestive of things in heaven. This theory is quite obviously operative in Vaughan's poem. Both doctrinally and historically there is much in the poem that could be examined in detail. Biographically, of course, we would need to know that Vaughan was a Welsh poet of the seventeenth century with mystical beliefs. As a Christian mystic believing in the theory of correspondence (quite popular, incidentally, in the seventeenth century), Vaughan would have very definite reasons for writing "The Water-Fall" and would not have introduced anything into the poem which lacked significance; we should have a generally objective approach in analysis, then, because we can not subjectively place ourselves in the position or beliefs of Vaughan.

The poem is a large metaphor—announced by the short title

—and if we confine ourselves to an analysis of that figure, attempt to amplify its meaning, and make some reference to Vaughan's beliefs and background, we will be able to interpret the poem with relatively little difficulty.

CASE 11:   JOHN DONNE'S "LOVERS' INFINITENESS"

If yet I have not all thy love,
Dear, I shall never have it all,
I cannot breathe one other sigh, to move,
Nor can entreat one other tear to fall,
And all my treasure, which should purchase thee,
Sighs, tears, and oaths, and letters I have spent.
Yet no more can be due to me,
Than at the bargain made was meant,
If then thy gift of love were partial,
That some to me, some should to others fall,
   Dear, I shall never have thee all.

Or if then thou gavest me all,
All was but all, which thou hadst then;
But if in thy heart, since, there be or shall,
New love created be, by other men,
Which have their stocks entire, and can in tears,
In sighs, in oaths, and letters outbid me,
This new love may beget new fears,
For, this love was not vow'd by thee.
And yet it was, thy gift being general,
The ground, thy heart is mine, what ever shall
   Gow there, dear, I should have it all.

Yet I would not have all yet,
He that hath all can have no more,
And since my love doth every day admit
New growth, thou shouldst have new rewards in store;
Thou canst not every day give me thy heart,
If thou canst give it, then thou never gavest it:
Love's riddles are, that though thy heart depart,
It stays at home, and thou with losing savest it:
But we will have a way more liberal,
Than changing hearts, to join them, so we shall
   Be one, and one another's All.

VERSIFICATION: Donne's poem has three eleven-line stanzas composed in the repeating pattern of a mixture of iambic tetrameter and iambic pentameter. The stanzaic rhyme scheme is the unusual: *ababcdcdeee*. It is fairly uncommon to have a triplet following eight lines of alternating rhyme. It is of course uncommon to find an eleven line stanza!

STRUCTURE BY PARADOX: The entire poem revolves around a series of paradoxes, each involving the speaker's desire to possess his lady's love in the fullest way possible. In the first stanza, the poet explains that if he does not yet have all his lady's love, then he shall never have it all. He is exhausted in his requests. He cannot sigh any more, nor cry, nor write more love letters. Furthermore, if she has decided to offer some of her love to others, there is simply no way in which he can have it all. It is a logical impossibility. In the second stanza, the poet explains that even if his lady had given him all her love *once,* she was only giving him that love which she then had; if, since then, she has felt new love for others, then he, the speaker, never had it *all* in a literal sense. In the third stanza, the poet explains one of the oldest paradoxes of all time: he does not *really* want all her love, because then there would be no rewards for his future endeavors. Even though the poet has previously stated that he has not the energy for future endeavors, he wishes that there be rewards for them. He wants and yet he does not want all his lady's love. He was given and yet was not really given all her love already. The confusion in the mind of the poet, his mixed and contradictory statements of what he desires, his absurd refusal to reconcile opposites, and his general attitude towards his achievement contribute to the total picture described by the title, "Lovers' Infiniteness." There really is no "all" to be had and we suspect that the poet somehow is aware of the absurdity of the term. There is the suggestion that all love is "infinite" and this is the effect which Donne hopes to produce. No matter how much love one has received from one's lady, one has not received it all, nor will one ever be able to receive it all. As the word "all" is repeated again and again, we realize that the poet is using the word as a synonym for "infiniteness."

POINT OF VIEW: We can describe, then, the composition of the poem, and the use of paradox to suggest the infiniteness of

love. What other ways are there in which to analyze the poem? What is the speaker's point of view? He seems to be one who has fallen in love—and stayed in love; one who has loved—and been loved; one who wants all his lady's love—and yet knows that he never will have it nor would he want to be able to have it. In short, the speaker's point of view partially explains the mystery of love. Donne is portraying, with great skill, a man in love. The combination of sounds and the repetition of the word "all" contribute to the confused, love-struck characterization of the speaker.

THEME: The *theme* of the poem is that love is infinite, that for real love to exist it must exist without dimension, without reference to time, space, or age. The speaker is presenting a subjective illustration of a theme which can be objectively discussed, particularly because we bring to our reading of his experience our own private experiences with love as well as our suspicions about love garnered from other poems and stories. As all love poets, Donne relies on figures and "gimmickry" (particularly his use of the word "all") to suggest the complexity and, more importantly, the lack of logic in love (thus his use of paradox). Through the combination of theme and style comes the rendition of one lover's confusing experience; the poem is successful because it conveys this experience imaginatively.

CASE 12: JOHN MASEFIELD'S "TEWKESBURY ROAD"

It is good to be out on the road, and going one knows not where,
    Going through meadow and village, one knows not whither
      nor why;
Through the grey light drift of the dust, in the keen cool rush
    of the air,
    Under the flying white clouds, and the broad blue lift of
    the sky.

And to halt at the chattering brook, in the tall green fern at
    the brink
    Where the harebell grows, and the gorse, and the foxgloves
    purple and white;
Where the shy-eyed delicate deer troop down to the brook
    to drink

When the stars are mellow and large at the coming on of
the night.
O, to feel the beat of the rain, and the homely smell of the earth,
Is a tune for the blood to jig to, a joy past power of words;
And the blessed green comely meadows are all a-ripple with
mirth
At the noise of the lambs at play and the dear wild cry
of the birds.

ENJOYING A POEM: When one reads a poem like this one
by John Masefield, one has the feeling that one is allowed to
respond to the poem in a quiet and contemplative way. The
poet is not asking us to analyze, to search for meaning, or even
to describe his poem. Rather, he wants us to join with him
in his imaginary trip. Each of us probably knows where there
is a Tewkesbury Road, a road where we can freely wander
along at our own pace and see the beauties of nature. When
we come to this poem, for example, our inclination is not to
analyze and describe but rather simply to discuss with sensitivity. We feel we should analyze a poem in the way a poet
would like it to be analyzed. Masefield would probably be content if we, as readers, understood the simple meaning of the
poem: wandering through nature is a rewarding experience.
The foxgloves, white clouds, and shy-eyed deer all fit together
perfectly in a picture of a natural and peaceful landscape. The
exact location of this landscape is unimportant, as are the
reasons that brought us there. What *is* important is that such
a landscape exists somewhere; and we must allow ourselves
time to discover it. The poem is similar to the smaller poem
on "leisure" we examined earlier in the chapter. Together they
remind us of the reasons we bother to analyze poetry at all.
There is a certain kind of experience which may be said to be
"poetic" which we all hunger after, both in life and in literature.
If we respond to such a poem subjectively, we are doing all that
is expected. Sometimes a poem needs to be "puzzled out."
Sometimes a poet presents a difficulty which we want to explore.
But as a final warning that not all poems are complex, and
neither are they all to be analyzed extensively, it seems fitting
to conclude the chapter with John Masefield's "Tewkesbury
Road."

ADVANCED ANALYSIS

In thinking about advanced analysis of poetry it is useful to consider the kinds of approaches available to us. What, in short, is the basic scope of this chapter? We can outline some of the necessary stages in advanced analysis:

I. ASKING MORE QUESTIONS: It will be pointed out that the key to advanced analysis is the process of asking more questions than one asks in ordinary or basic analysis.

II. ESTABLISHING BASIC MEANING: It is important to remember that before one can discuss the complex aspects of a poem, one must still begin by outlining the poem's basic meaning. Even in advanced analysis it is essential to begin with what is easiest and proceed in an orderly way to what is more complex. In advanced analysis one is simply going to proceed *further;* this does not automatically imply that one can start further along the analytical path.

III. PROBING THE LESS OBVIOUS: The first "real" stage of advanced analysis. When one has covered the preliminary essentials one then enters the area where there are problems and questions which have no obvious answers.

IV. STRUCTURE AND MEANING: One area in which to begin advanced analysis is the exploration of the subtle and often delicately established relationship between a poem's structure and meaning; how does the organization and composition of the poem correspond to the idea of the poem?

V. STRUCTURE AND IMAGERY: In connection with the relationship between structure and meaning we often try to explore the development of patterns of imagery within a poem; in order to amplify the presentation of idea, the poet arranges his images in a deliberate way.

VI. MAKING ANALYSIS PARALLEL COMPLEXITY: When we think about the poem being analyzed, we must always keep asking ourselves how we can best make our analysis correspond to the particular complexities of the poem.

VII. DETERMINING THE STYLE: One of the most difficult tasks of the critic is to explain the *style* of the poet. This is done through a detailed exploration of all the discernible elements of the writer's methods of composition. This exploration further demands evaluation of the effectiveness of the style which the poet has chosen for his task.

VIII. STYLISTIC DEVICES: Certain methods of composition are referred to as "stylistic devices"; in the analysis of a passage from Milton we can see, for example, how simile and allusion are used to expand the narrative while at the same time elision, latinization, and varied accent are used to contract the narrative. The result is a balanced style.

IX. LITERARY DEBT: It is often useful or necessary to investigate a poet's literary indebtedness to other poets. What, we inquire further, are the *sources* for a particular poem. Exploring literary debts is basically an extension of the historical approach introduced in the last chapter.

X. SYMBOLISM: The ultimate task of advanced analysis is to explain the poet's use of symbols and, further, to explain how the symbols work together with the *images* to amplify the meaning of the poem. Tracing the poet's establishment of a pattern of symbolism is one of the most difficult problems of all analysis; we must attempt to understand the precise ways in which the poet substitutes the real world, or objects from the real world, for the unreal, invisible world.

We will now turn our attention to a more detailed discussion of these various aspects of advanced analysis.

ASKING MORE QUESTIONS: One should be able to analyze

almost any poem by adhering to the different approaches introduced in our discussion of fundamental approaches and exemplified in the case studies. Sometimes, however, a student wishes to pursue the meaning of a poem even further and it becomes necessary to ask more questions. It can not be stressed too heavily that analyzing poetry is asking questions about poetry. When we direct our thoughts to the nature of advanced analysis we realize that we are simply thinking about asking more advanced questions. To analyze poetry to the fullest extent is to ask every possible question that comes to mind. Instead of talking about a pattern of imagery we decide to inquire about the nature of every image in a poem and about the relationship which we can see between as many of them as possible. Instead of outlining the cardinal points of a doctrine we present the doctrine in its entirety. Instead of thinking about the psychological implications of a poem we present the archetypal pattern which the psychology suggests.

UNLIMITED ANALYSIS: There is virtually no limit to the extent of analysis for there are always more questions to be asked and possible answers found. Comparisons can always be extended, and research can always uncover something more of historical, etymological, or biographical importance. We can follow the Jungian bases of archetypal analysis and inquire whether we are giving intellectual or emotional consent to ideas and characters. We can analyze our own feelings until we have determined exactly why we feel the way we do about almost every word and idea in a poem. Analysis, then, is always an "unfinished business." We can ask almost as many questions about a poem as we can ask about ourselves.

To illustrate the process of questioning, let us examine a very short poem by Emily Dickinson, "Hope is the thing with feathers":

> Hope is the thing with feathers
> That perches in the soul,
> And sings the tune without the words,
> And never stops at all.
>
> And sweetest in the gale is heard;
> And sore must be the storm

That could abash the little bird
That kept so many warm.

I've heard it in the chillest land,
And on the strangest sea;
Yet, never, in extremity,
It asked a crumb of me.

ESTABLISHING BASIC MEANING: To begin with, we can pass over the problems of versification and discuss the poem's meaning. What is the poem *about?* Basically we can see that Emily Dickinson is writing about hope; her theme is that hope sits in each of us like a curious bird and keeps singing to us in times of despair while at the same time never asking for anything in return. The theme then might be paraphrased: human beings are blessed with hope, a gift they receive for free which guides them through hard times.

PROBING THE LESS OBVIOUS: Now we can begin asking questions with less obvious answers. For example, why is hope a "thing" rather than a bird? We think of it as a bird after we have read the poem; why then has the poetess so deliberately refrained from referring to a bird? It is possible that she wanted to suggest the fact that we do not really know what hope looks like. We only know that it exists; we have never seen it. Although it may seem like a bird—it perches, it has feathers, it sings, etc.—we do not know what kind of bird it seems *most* like. Perhaps all of this is being suggested in the one word, "thing." But this is only one small part of the mystery in the poem. Why is the tune without words? Is it, like the "thing," unrecognizable? Are there no lyrics in hope? Why does Dickinson bother to tell us whether or not the tune which the thing sings has words or not? Why does she think it should matter?

The key to advanced analysis is to keep asking questions even when one feels he has asked enough questions. To pursue our inquiry into Emily Dickinson's twelve-line poem further, why does the thing which represents hope never stop singing? In the second stanza the poetess introduces the possibility that hope could be destroyed, although whatever could destroy hope would have to be "sore." Is there any inconsistency between the constant singing and the possibility of no song? Or is the poetess trying purposely to suggest the dangers surrounding some "thing" apparently as invincible as hope? Notice that the bird-like thing's song is "sweetest" in the gale or time of trouble. That is, hope rallies most when hope is most needed; hope responds to despair consistently (if perhaps enigmatically). There is virtually no limit to the number of questions we can ask. Why do we find the word "sore?" Why "chillest?" Each word has been selected from many possibilities, so we should try to determine why a poet chooses one word rather than another. We will always be able to ask more questions than we will be able to answer, but also, to answer more questions than we originally thought we would be able to answer.

STRUCTURE AND MEANING: While one should bear in mind the importance of asking more and more questions, one should also realize that a large part of advanced analysis is concerned with the relationship between form and content, or between structure and meaning. What kind of meaning does the form itself have? And why is a particular form used to convey a certain category of meaning? Granted, not every poem can be discussed in these terms. Sometimes there simply is no important relationship between the structure and the meaning of a poem. When one is attempting to analyze a poem fully, one should try to determine at the outset whether or not there is in fact a case to be made at all. What kind of *development* does the poem have? A poem has various components put together in a particular way for certain reasons. Analysis attempts to demonstrate why a poem is constructed as it is and why it is or is not effective.

How does the structure relate to the presentation of the central idea? Does the main idea come in the opening, the middle, or the end of the poem? If it comes early, how does the material which follows relate to it? If it comes late, how does the material which precedes it develop into it? In other words, there is always some way of explaining the relationship between the meaning and the way in which the poem is put together.

John Donne's poem "A Lecture Upon The Shadow" presents a good opportunity to discuss structure and meaning:

Stand still, and I will read to thee
A Lecture, love, in Loves philosophy.
    These three houres that we have spent,
    Walking here, Two shadowes went
Along with us, which we our selves produc'd;
 But, now the Sunne is just above our head,
    We doe those shadowes tread;
    And to brave clearness all things are reduc'd.
  So whilst our infant loves did grow,
  Disguises did, and shadowes, flow,
  From us, and our cares; but, now 'tis not so.

That love hath not attain'd the high'st degree,
Which is still diligent lest others see.

Except our loves at this noone stay,
We shall new shadowes make the other way.
    As the first were made to blinde
    Others; these which come behinde
Will work upon our selves, and blind our eyes.
If our loves faint, and westwardly decline;
    To me thou, falsly, thine,
    And I to thee mine actions shall disguise.

  The morning shadowes weare away,
  But these grow longer all the day,
  But oh, loves day is short, if love decay.

Love is a growing, or full constant light;
And his first minute, after noone, is night.

This is without doubt a difficult poem and must be read several times before we can even begin to answer our own question of how the structure relates to the presentation of the central idea. In this poem Donne subtly contrasts perfect and imperfect love. The device he uses to make the comparison is an evolutionary pattern of "shadowe" imagery. The thought of the poem is geometrically constructed; as in a triangle, young love is at one point, mature love at a second—the apex—and faded love at a third. The development of these three temporal stages of love leads into the central theme which is summarized in the final couplet: "Love is a growing, or full constant light;/

and his first minute, after noone, is night." In other words, once love spoils a little bit, it will be ruined eventually.

DIVIDING THE POEM THROUGH STRUCTURE AND IMAGERY: Donne develops three progressive stages of love: young, or early, love which is—by definition—the beginning of a partnership. This immature and somewhat skeptical love expands into a mature love in which mutual honesty and affection are at their apex; this perfect love then passes into a dying love, the fearful stage of a romance where doubts are spawned and insincerity increases. The middle stage is perfection while the first and last stages are imperfections.

Perfection and imperfection are characterized by full brightness and full darkness respectively. Donne varies the light imagery between these two extremes in order to establish the mood and to delineate the differing characteristics of the three stages of love. The poem is organized in a way which will most clearly establish each stage of love with the symbolically correct amount of light. Mature and perfect love is revealed at noontime when the sun is directly overhead; there are no shadows, no darkness, and thus no imperfections. Early love has minor shadows which disappear; these morning shadows—the inherent imperfections of young love—have had their major effect upon others; the afternoon shadows, in contrast,—the deeper imperfections which result from self-imposed doubts and perhaps pride—have the effect of injuring the lovers themselves. The steadily lengthening afternoon shadows represent the progressive decay of waning love; they reflect the parasitic nature of unwarranted suspicions which eat away the purity of a romance.

The entire structure of the poem is designed to make the coming and going of daylight symbolically parallel to the coming and going of love. Donne feels that once one departs from the perfect love symbolized by high noon, one might as well move to the complete imperfection symbolized by total darkness (night). As soon as a tiny shadow appears after noon-time, it will grow and ultimately bring about the total replacement of light and of love; thus the "first minute, after noone, is night." The poem has a geometry, a symmetrical development. Through a tightly controlled logic, Donne relates his structure to his meaning. We are forced to ask various questions about the imagery in the poem. The more we inquire into the imagery of light and darkness, the more we realize how well organized the poem is in its entirety. The *idea* of the poem has been effectively presented by presenting a large analogy between love and daylight. By using the shadow images, Donne has been able to fashion a geometrical structure through which he can skillfully contrast the three recognizable stages of love.

ANALYSIS PARALLELS COMPLEXITY: It should be clear after reading Donne's poem, that this kind of complicated poem can easily be discussed in terms of structure and meaning. If a certain structure has obviously been chosen in order to demonstrate an idea, and if the relationship between the two is then immediately visible, there is little room for speculation. A more complex poem responds more fully to analysis. Simple ideas presented in simple ways do not require deep analysis. Poems which are complicated or ambiguous require more advanced and persistent analysis than poems which are relatively easy to understand. One must somehow "sense" the point beyond which it is frivolous to keep asking questions. Granted, it never hurts to keep asking questions, but one must exercise a certain amount of judgement in trying to *predict the extent of analysis* which will be required. If one has some idea of how much questioning and examining one is going to do, one will not fall into the familiar trap of saying as much as possible and then suddenly stopping.

STYLE: In analyzing poetry we often turn to considerations of literary style. The term *style* is fairly inclusive and denotes simultaneously such concepts as "diction," "figurative language," and "rhetorical" constructions. Style refers to the whole formed by the writer's techniques and his selection of words. There are often certain "secrets" to a writer's style which can only be recognized and understood by way of relatively extensive analysis. To discuss the style of a poet one must first have surveyed all of the nuances and subtleties of the writer's kind of expression. Discussion of style calls for generalizations supported by particulars.

DETERMINING THE KIND OF STYLE: In literature there are a good many kinds of style which have come to be known by particular adjectives. The style of every poet is unique, for style is a way of referring to the poet's originality of expression, but we can often refer to a kind of style. For example, to say that a poet writes in the "Miltonic" style means that he uses a lofty, grand form of expression *similar* to, but not the same as, that of Milton. We speak of a poem's being written in a "low" style, meaning in a humble, unadorned way. We use labels such as these to associate a poet with either the style of another poet or of another school of poetry. We never use a label as a complete and final description.

Discussing style quite naturally leads one into very difficult problems of evaluating the effectiveness of the poet's chosen ways of expressing himself. To judge a style we must first understand its precise originality. We must familiarize ourselves with the poet's rhythm, emphasis, and organization of ideas and images. We can keep in mind Jonathan Swift's definition of good style as "proper words in proper places"; however, it is quite another matter to decide what is or is not "proper." Discussions of literary style, then, lead one into more advanced analysis. Obviously if a term such as "style" *includes* many other terms—all of which need to be mentioned and explained —it requires more time than any few of the terms by themselves.

Sometimes a poet is able to combine several seemingly incompatible techniques within his style of poetic composition. For the purposes of discussion, let us examine a passage from Milton's *Paradise Lost*. If the reader does not remember some of the terms used in the discussion—such as simile, allusion, etc.—he is urged to return to their meanings outlined in the third chapter. The passage by Milton follows: the confrontation of Satan and Death in Book II, lines 704-720:

> So spake the grisly terror, and in shape,
> So speaking and so threat'ning, grew tenfold
> More dreadful and deform: on th'other side
> Incens't with indignation Satan stood
> Unterrifi'd, and like a Comet burned,
> That fires the length of *Ophiucus* huge
> In th'Artic Sky, and from his horrid hair
> Shakes Pestilence and War. Each at the Head

Levell'd his deadly aim; thir fatal hands
No second stroke intend, and such a frown
Each cast at th'other, as when two black Clouds
With Heav'n's Artillery fraught, come rattling on
Over the *Caspian,* then stand front to front
Hov'ring a space, till Winds the signal blow
To join thir dark Encounter in mid air:
So frown'd the mighty Combatants, that Hell
Grew darker at thir frown, so matcht they stood.

STYLISTIC DEVICES

A. EXPANSION THROUGH SIMILE AND ALLUSION: This passage most noticeably exemplifies two of Milton's most basic tools for *stylistic expansion:* the use of *simile* and the use of *classical allusions*. Both tools serve to widen the context of the setting, accounting for what some critics have called the "grandeur" or "elevation" of Milton's style. In examining Milton's style, one is always aware of two basic techniques: expansion and contraction. Milton expands his situations—through simile and allusion—in order that they may acquire a more universal quality and leave the reader with a more grandiose sense experience. In order to offset the requirements of such an expansive panorama, Milton contracts his rhetoric by employing a rather complex, abbreviated syntax.

There are two strong similes in the passage, one introduced by the word "like," and the other by the word "as."

> Satan stood
> Unterrifi'd, and like a Comet burn'd,
> That fires the length of *Ophiucus* huge
> In th'Artic Sky . . .

This simile comparing Satan to a burning comet speeding through the Artic sky immediately *magnifies* the visual portrait of Satan: he is no longer a spirit; he is an omnipotent ball of flame. To reinforce the expanding image of Satan, Milton points out that the comet fires the length of Ophiucus which is one of the largest northern constellations. Milton has carefully enlarged the size of the setting to astronomical proportions and enlarged the scope of the reader's experience, alluding to the classical understanding of the constellation's meaning.

In examining the second large simile of the passage, one finds Milton using the same technique which he employed in the first:

> and such a frown
> Each cast at th'other, as when two black Clouds
> With Heav'n's Artillery fraught, came rattling on
> Over the *Caspian* . . .

In this simile Milton is comparing the frowns of Satan and Death to two stormy clouds about to collide; he has *magnified* their expressions by relating them to things more colossal. As before, he has strengthened his simile by a classical allusion: the clouds collide over the Caspian sea which, as early as Horace (*Odes,*II,9.12), was proverbially stormy. The classical allusion strengthens the vivid picture of the dark, raging frowns of two opponents about to engage in combat. In both of the large images examined, then, simile and classical allusion have converged effectively to enlarge a picture into a more spectacular panorama. And such forceful, expressionistic, visual imagery dominates the greater part of the Miltonic narrative. By reinforcing his similes with names such as Ophiucus and Caspian Milton helps transport the reader around the world.

B. CONTRACTION THROUGH VARIED ACCENT, ELISION, AND LATINIZATION: While expanding the reader's experience, Milton must be careful not to allow the narrative to become too lengthy and tedious; he avoids this by *varying his stress pattern,* using frequent *elisions,* and by *transposing the word order (latinization).* Using iambic pentameter, the last syllable of each line is heavily stressed; to stress further the conclusion of each line, Milton usually ends each line with a long harsh monosyllable (e.g., "shape," "side," "hair," "head," "Clouds," etc.) In order to place a greater percentage of heavy stress throughout the passage as a whole, Milton frequently contracts syllables and eliminates unneeded vowels. In this passage Milton has elided about twelve vowels and syllables; for example, he has made threatening "threat'ning"; the other, "th'other"; the Arctic, "th'Artic"; Heaven's "Heav'n's"; hovering, "hov'ring." In each of these instances he has contracted the expression to a minimum length and thereby increased the capacity of the line for carrying heavy stress; in this fashion Milton has allowed for more vigorous "hearing" of the poetry than could otherwise be achieved. Some of his elisions, however, could be said to be unnecessary. For example, there is no apparent reason (aside from stylistic habit) to change unterrified to "unterrifi'd," or burned to "burn'd." He has not contracted his meter; he has not allowed for additional stress.

In this passage we find another characteristic technique of contraction: latinization. Milton employs a Latin syntax; in several instances he places the main verb after its direct object as in "till winds the signal blow." Another type of latinization is positioning the adjective after the substantive, as illustrated here by "Comet burn'd." The use of the ablative absolute is also common; however, it is quite difficult to find without meticulous scrutiny. An example here is, "on th'other side/ Incens't with indignation." (The ablative absolute is an independent clause in the ablative case—the case which expresses source, cause, agency and instrument, also deprivation—used to express time, cause, or circumstance.)

SUMMARY: A BALANCED STYLE: In summary of our review of the style of the passage, we can clearly see that Milton establishes an equilibrium between complexity of syntax and simplicity of broad, allusive imagination; a balance exists between his techniques of expansion and those of contraction. By the use of epic simile and classical allusion, he expands the sensations; by the use of elisions and latinization, he contracts his rhetoric and maintains continuity. Now, not every passage of poetry could be so extensively analyzed in terms of style. Again the reader must begin by attempting to predict the extent of analysis which will be required in order to explain the poet's style. It may be relatively easy to demonstrate that the poet is writing in a style based on pretentious mannerisms, or in a style designed to be humorous, etc. This is not to say that only serious poets write in styles requiring extensive examination; every poet must be treated individually and his style must speak for itself. The recognizable elements of style will either be difficult and complicated or they will be simple and unadorned. The subtleties of style—as, for example, Milton's sometime use of unnecessary elisions—require more subtle comment. The more sophisticated a style is, the more sophisticated one's analysis should be. And while it is important to recognize difference, it is sometimes equally important to recognize sameness. This leads us to our next consideration.

LITERARY DEBT: It should be mentioned briefly here that poets are not uncommonly "indebted" to one another in some particular way; furthermore, poets have debts to ideas and philosophical systems. In other words, any corpus of ideas regarding either content or expression from which a poet "borrows" constitutes an area where he owes a debt. We speak of Milton's debt to Greek tragedy when discussing *Samson Agonistes,* Milton's play and the first Greek tragedy in English. We speak of Spenser's debt to Chaucer because Spenser drew many ideas from his predecessor. Whether we speak of Eliot's debt to Yeats, or Wordsworth's debt to Coleridge, we are always concerned with a relationship between the poet and some other body of knowledge from which he has borrowed. It follows that a certain kind of literary analysis addresses itself to the question of indebtedness. We can analyze a poem by trying to discover phrases, images, conventions, themes, etc., which a poet has apparently "borrowed" from somewhere else. No other kind of analysis becomes as much of a detective game as the analysis of literary debts.

SOURCES: We search relentlessly after the "sources" of an idea or an image which we have seen in a poem and which for some reason or another we feel did not originate with the author of that particular poem. Sometimes the stimulus is merely a matter of our saying to ourselves that we have seen that phrase somewhere else—and thus a search begins for the source. Many poets, and most of the good ones, acknowledge their indebtedness to certain of their predecessors (and sometimes to their contemporaries); they are fully aware of the convention that dictates that one acknowledge his sources. There is no question of "plagiarism" in legitimate, acknowledged borrowing. Most theoretical critics have stressed the importance of studying the past masters. Through imitation of techniques, an aspiring poet can learn a great deal. This does not give aspiring poets free license to borrow words and images extensively from poets of wide reputation, but rather to acknowledge that they have learned from better poets; they are, in short, "indebted" to them.

GUESSWORK AND SOURCES: Sometimes critics are only able to speculate regarding sources; that is, a case can often be made for an existing "debt" without substantiation in fact. When we *know* that one poet read another poet's work the task is infinitely easier than when we only suspect that he must have read them. For example, many articles have been written discussing the similarity between Henry Vaughan's poem "The Retreat" and Wordsworth's poem, "Ode, Intimations of Immortality from Recollections of Early Childhood." Vaughan's poem, written in the seventeenth century, opens in this way:

> Happy those early days! when I
> Shin'd in my Angel-infancy.
> Before I understood this place
> Appointed for my second race,
> Or taught my soul to fancy ought
> But a white, celestial thought,
> When yet I had not walkt above
> A mile, or two, from my first love . . .

The poem by Wordsworth, written in the early nineteenth century, suggests that Wordsworth somehow had become familiar with Vaughan's poem; Wordsworth begins:

> There was a time when meadow, grove, and stream,
> The earth, and every common sight,
>   To me did seem
>   Apparelled in celestial light,
> The glory and the freshness of a dream.
> It is not new as it hath been of yore;—
>   Turn whereso'er I may,
>   By night or day,
> The things which I have seen I now can see no more.

That Wordsworth's poem should contain in the opening stanza a reference to celestial light similar to that in "The Retreat" suggests that Vaughan's poem may have been one of Wordsworth's *sources*. Wordsworth, in other words, may owe a "debt" to Vaughan. But, as Wordsworth's poem concludes differently and as we have no way of proving whether or not

Wordsworth read Vaughan's poem, the question of indebtedness will always be just a question—unless some researcher discovers some fact hitherto unknown about a possible relationship between Wordsworth and Vaughan.

There are literally innumerable cases of both concrete, positive and possible, uncertain literary indebtedness. Through analysis of a poem's relationship to something else we are able to better understand the poem in question. By continuously searching for proof of suspected relationships between poets and schools of poetry we broaden the whole fabric of literary history and thus our critical background. The more we understand a poet's debts and sources, the more we understand a poet.

SYMBOLISM: Many poems are based on symbolic statement. The poet offers something on the concrete level which symbolizes something either on the abstract level or on another, unstated concrete level. When we discuss symbolism in poetry we are concerned with the representation of one world by another.

SYMBOL AND IMAGE: All of the things we have been discussing in this chapter have been connected in one way or another to imagery and patterns of imagery. How a poet uses images is part of his unique style. When do we decide that something is no longer an image and instead a symbol? The usual answer is that if some picture or representation is repeated over and over again it becomes a symbol; if a poet uses the word "sun" every time he obviously is speaking about goodness, the sun may be said to be a *symbol of* goodness. If there is some sunlight in the background setting every time something good happens, or if sunlight is, in any way, consistently associated with good, we can speak as well about the symbolism of sunlight.

SUBSTITUTING THE REAL FOR AN UNREAL WORLD: Poets who express themselves symbolically usually think in terms of another invisible world which can never be literally experienced. Instead they feel that it can be symbolized by objects and visible things in this real and concrete world; the poet wants to suggest imaginatively what the other world is like and this resort to our present world is the only way in which he can make that suggestion. In many poems there is a "correspondence" between terrestrial and celestial objects; that is, things on this earth and familiar to us are used to symbolize things not on this earth and therefore not familiar to us. As most mystics and extremely religious poets are busy trying to imagine ways of symbolizing the "beyond," it is natural that their poetry should contain the most symbols.

Imagery is somewhat generalized while symbolism is particular. We can refer to the symbolism of water in T. S. Eliot's "The Waste Land" or to the moon symbolism in Shakespeare's history plays and some of Yeats' poetry. Symbols are concrete and recognizable; they are as emblematic and visual as images are sometimes only suggestive and even vague. Some symbols have been used again and again and thus by this use have become "archetypes" in literature. That is, because of the entire situation in the Garden of Eden, lush gardens have a suggestion of natural splendor and innocence while snakes usually symbolize threatening evil and an apple seduction or temptation, etc. Each of the objects in the Garden, and the Garden itself, has become an archetypal symbol.

ESTABLISHING SYMBOLISM: A poet can symbolize in very deliberate and recognizable ways. If, in the world of a poem, every person becomes associated either with an animal of prey or with an animal which preys, a large symbolic world of hunting is created. Each character in the poem can become a member of either the hunters or the hunted as the poem comes slowly to symbolize a large jungle. We can speak of the way a writer uses *images* to establish patterns of symbolism, because *images reinforce symbols*. Imagery contributes to the mood or atmosphere in which the symbols can best be recognized and understood. When we mention archetypes we should be careful to realize that there are *public symbols* and *private symbols*. That is, some symbols, through repeated use, have the same connotations whenever they occur; others, in contrast, are products of a particular poet's imagination and remain fairly mysterious. If a poet has a private symbol it often remains private unless, or until, someone decides that it has some particular meaning which becomes clear when one has observed carefully how the symbol functions in every poem in which it is discovered.

In order to show how mechanically symbols can operate on one level, let us briefly examine George Herbert's "Virtue":

> Sweet day, so cool, so calm, so bright!
>   The bridal of the earth and sky—
> The dew shall weep thy fall to-night;
>   For thou must die.
>
> Sweet rose, whose hue angry and brave
>   Bids the rash gazer wipe his eye,
> Thy root is ever in its grave,
>   And thou must die.
>
> Sweet spring, full of sweet days and roses,
> A box where sweets compacted lie,
> My music shows ye have your closes,
>   And all must die.
>
> Only a sweet and virtuous soul,
> Like season'd timber, never gives;
> But though the whole world turn to coal,
>   Then chiefly lives.

In Herbert's poem, the day of the first stanza, the rose of the second stanza, and the spring of the third all *symbolize* impermanence or mutability. All three will literally pass away and yet the important point is that some things do pass away while virtue, in contradistinction, can be permanent. This is the point of the poem and it is forcefully stated through the use of symbols.

ADVANCED ANALYSIS: In thinking about what constitutes advanced analysis, we should merely be thinking about what constitutes advanced poetry. In other words, if a poem involves symbols it is more advanced than a poem which does not involve symbols. If a poem has an advanced and sophisticated structure and relationship between structure and meaning, it will be more difficult to analyze than one which has a simple structure and a simple relationship between structure and meaning. If a poem has complexities of style or has obvious "sources" which need to be examined, it will obviously require more advanced analysis than one which has neither. The more ways in which a poem may be said to be "complex" or "advanced," the more ways in which the critic will have to examine the poem. In the following chapter we will look at some poems which present a greater difficulty than the earlier ones we examined. The kind of difficulty will vary from one poem to another.

CASE EXAMPLES

CASE 1: ROBERT BROWNING'S "MEETING AT NIGHT" AND "PARTING AT MORNING"

MEETING AT NIGHT

I.

The grey sea and the long black land;
And the yellow half-moon large and low;
And the startled little waves that leap
In fiery ringlets from their sleep,
As I gain the cove with pushing prow,
And quench its speed i' the slushy sand.

II.

Then a mile of warm sea-scented beach;
Three fields to cross till a farm appears;
A tap at the pane, the quick sharp scratch
And blue spurt of a lighted match,
And a voice less loud, thro' its joys and fears,
Than the two hearts beating each to each!

PARTING AT MORNING

Round the cape of a sudden came the sea,
And the sun looked over the mountain's rim:
And straight was a path of gold for him,
And the need of a world of men for me.

DEVELOPING THE ROMANTIC EXPERIENCE: Browning's pair of short poems constitutes a very delicate kind of poetic composition. There is no overstatement; everything is relatively subdued but does not lack force. There is a certain sophistication to the poem perhaps not seen at first in simple analysis. The first poem is a series of impressionistic details registered as a man goes to meet secretly with the woman he loves. The setting is delicately formed through reference to a night-time romantic landscape—the gray sea and the long dark land are easily pictured by anyone who has been off-shore in a boat at night. The yellow half-moon provides just enough (but not too much) light to illuminate the shore and the little, tiny waves which roll endlessly into the small cove. The young man brings his boat into the cove and comes to a halt as he reaches the sand. The first half of his journey is complete. He now must walk along a mile of beach which gives off the scent of the sea; now he must cross through three fields until he reaches a farm. Once at the farm he taps on the glass and furtively enters. All we learn about the actual union with his lover is the murmur of talk and the rapid beating of two hearts. *Most* of the romantic experience is contained in the anticipation, in riding in the boat, walking along the beach, and crossing through the fields. The actual love-experience is very brief; Browning has very subtly made that love seem more beautiful by saying very little about it. His earlier description is filled with a lover's anticipation and there is a fully sophisticated approach to the romance.

STYLE AND STRUCTURE: The style in which the poem is written is one of suggestiveness, of letting a few small details carry most of the narration and importance of the poem. There is a strong relationship between structure and meaning, for Browning has, on the one hand, made the poem appropriately short, and, on the other, made it very climactic; the poem is structured so that the small characteristics of the event lead up to—and suddenly conclude in—his union with the lover. We can see that the simplicity of structure, and its climactic nature, make it very appropriate for what the poem is about.

ANTI-ROMANTIC STATEMENT: The second poem, designed of course to be spoken by the voice of the first poem, is much shorter. This is fitting because the major part of love, as the structure of Browning's first poem suggested, lies in the anticipation rather than in the aftermath. The joy in the furtive boat ride through the moonlit night and the walk along the beach have a much more exotic potentiality than the parting, the return in the morning sunlight. In this second poem the narrator is departing from the cove he entered the night before and as he sees the ocean he comments that he needs a world of men once again. This is basically and unequivocally an anti-romantic statement; the speaker experiences what is at least a small revulsion against the great moment with his lover the night before. In another sense, however, the second poem is romantic for it makes the experience of joy in anticipation even that much brighter by contrast. The romance of what led up to union is made stronger by the fact that what follows is weak. Thus there is a double suggestion of both love and anti-love and the poem becomes slightly ambiguous without ever becoming a complete mystery.

STRUCTURE AND MEANING: As in the first poem, "Meeting at Night," in the sequel poem Browning has allowed structure to parallel meaning; as there is much less meaning in the parting at morning, the poem is much shorter; it is brief, just as the emotions of parting are thin. The varied sensory responses to the romantic evening landscape in the first poem are now only matched by the one, almost gruff statement that the narrator feels like returning once again to a world of men. In short, in both poems we discover an appropriate and sophisticated relationship among components of various natures; in form and style the poem should be considered successful.

CASE 2: DRYDEN'S ODE, "A SONG FOR ST. CECILIA'S DAY"

I.

From harmony, from heav'nly harmony
   This universal frame began:
   When Nature underneath a heap
     Of jarring atoms lay,
   And could not heave her head,
The tuneful voice was heard from high:
   "Arise, ye more than dead."
Then cold, and hot, and moist, and dry,
   In order to their stations leap,
     And Music's pow'r obey.

From harmony, from heav'nly harmony
   This universal frame began:
   From harmony to harmony
Thro' all the compass of the notes it ran,
The diapson closing full in Man.

II.

What passion cannot Music raise and quell!
   When Jubal struck the corded shell,
   His list'ning brethren stood around,
   And, wond'ring, on their faces fell
   To worship that celestial sound.
Less than a god they thought there could not dwell
   Within the hollow of that shell
   That spoke so sweetly and so well.
What passion cannot Music raise and quell!

III.

   The trumpet's loud clangor
      Excites us to arms,
   With shrill notes of anger,
      And mortal alarms.
   The double double double beat
      Of the thund'ring Drum
Cries: "Hark! the foes come;
Charge, charge, 't is too late to retreat."

IV.

   The soft complaining Flute
   In dying notes discovers
   The woes of hopeless lovers,
Whose dirge is whisper'd by the warbling Lute.

V.

   Sharp Violins proclaim
Their jealous pangs, and desperation,
Fury, frantic indignation,
Depth of pains, and height of passion,
   For the fair, disdainful dame.

VI.

But O! what art can teach,
What human voice can reach,
The sacred Organ's praise?
Notes inspiring holy love,
Notes that wing their heav'nly ways
To mend the choirs above.

VII.

Orpheus could lead the savage race;
And trees unrooted left their place,
Sequacious of the lyre;
But bright Cecilia rais'd the wonder high'r:
When to her Organ vocal breath was giv'n,
An angel heard, and straight appear'd,
Mistaking earth for heav'n.

GRAND CHORUS

As from the pow'r of sacred lays
The spheres began to move,
And sung the great Creator's praise
To all the blest above;
So, when the last and dreadful hour
This crumbling pageant shall devour,
The trumpet shall be heard on high,
The dead shall live, the living die,
And Music shall untune the sky.

HISTORICAL APPROACH: From a historical point of view, one
would need to mention that a London musical society had
started the custom of celebrating November 22, the feast of
St. Cecilia (the patroness of music), five years before it asked
Dryden to contribute this ode in 1687. The subject of Dryden's
ode, thereby naturally associated with a celebration of music,
is an explanation of the classical idea that the universe achieves
an overall harmony through the presence of opposing, clashing
elements. This harmony through clashing suggests the approach
of stylistic analysis, for again we find a strong relationship between form and meaning or structure and content.

ESTABLISHING BASIC MEANING: It is appropriate when writing a musical ode to strive for musical effects in the words and in the versification. Before turning to this consideration, however, let us summarize briefly what the poem is about. Dryden first explains the central idea in the background of the poem that the world was created in harmony. He then explains the power of music to stir the passions—which leads naturally into the evocative description of several musical instruments. The point is that no one other instrument can equal the organ—the vocal sounds of Cecilia which directed an angel toward the earth instead of heaven. In the final chorus we are told that when the last trumpet blows, ending the existence of the universe, the music of the spheres will also cease and the sky will be "untuned."

STYLISTIC DEVICES: MUSICAL EFFECTS: Dryden achieves great musical effects, particularly in the central section of the poem when he moves carefully from one instrument to another with corresponding changes in versification. The bold pronouncement of the trumpets captures perfectly the blaring sounds which they make: "The trumpet's loud clangor/ Excites us to arms." And then the sounds of the flute are crystallized in the same fashion; the words parallel the meaning as much as they convey meaning when Dryden writes, "The soft complaining Flute/ In dying notes discovers/ The woes of hopeless lovers." In other words, Dryden has not simply written an ode celebrating the powers of music; rather he has *demonstrated* a host of musical sounds through his presentation of harmony on the one hand and of separate musical instruments on the other. Thus Dryden seems to have captured the very essence of music. It was, not unexpectedly, set to music, first by the Italian composer Draghi, and eventually in the eighteenth century by Handel. Part of the musical effect of the poem stems naturally from the repetition of the phrase, "From harmony, from heav'nly harmony." By referring repeatedly *to* harmony we are made to feel we are somehow participating *in* harmony. Other repetitions—"What passion cannot Music raise and quell"—remind us of the use of musical repetition in orchestrated works, while the suggested sounds of single instruments like the trumpet and flute remind us that harmony is, in any final analysis, created out of the combination of discordant sounds.

EVALUATING THE POEM: One of Dryden's early major critics, Joseph Warton, praised the poem for its succession of a variety of passions and feelings, the overall melody which is sustained throughout, and the appropriateness of the diction; the only part of the poem he objected to is the conclusion, specifically the last four lines which he thought were somehow too epigramatic. Other critics have found objections to the antithetical coupling of music and "untuning" (Samuel Johnson was one reader annoyed by this part of the poem); however, it is easy to see this ending as an appropriate way of referring back to the opening statement about the way in which the universe had been created in harmony.

SUMMARY: The poem, all in all, has a subtle relationship between sound and meaning, and between form and content. The poem uses different kinds of stanzas and rhyme patterns and yet as a whole sounds harmonious; and this is what the poem is about. In other words, Dryden has demonstrated the very idea of the poem; style parallels meaning; structure supports theme. The tight organization of contrasting parts into a melodic and sweet-sounding whole requires very delicate poetic composition and Dryden seems to have obtained it perfectly.

CASE 3: EDGAR ALLAN POE'S "ANNABEL LEE"

It was many and many a year ago,
    In a kingdom by the sea,
That a maiden there lived whom you may know
    By the name of Annabel Lee.
And this maiden she lived with no other thought
    Than to love and be loved by me.

She was a child and I was a child
    In this kingdom by the sea:
But we loved with a love that was more than love—
    I and my Annabel Lee,
With a love that the winged seraphs of heaven
    Coveted her and me.

And this was the reason that, long ago,
    In this kingdom by the sea,
A wind blew out of a cloud, chilling

My beautiful Annabel Lee,
So that her high-born kinsmen came
    And bore her away from me,
To shut her up in a sepulchre
    In this kingdom by the sea.

The angels, not half so happy in heaven,
    Went envying her and me—
Yes! that was the reason (as all men know,
    In this kingdom by the sea)
That the wind came out of the cloud one night,
    Chilling and killing my Annabel Lee.

But our love it was stronger by far than the love
    Of those who were older than we—
    Of many far wiser than we—
And neither the angels in heaven above,
    Nor the demons down under the sea,
Can ever dissever my soul from the soul
    Of the beautiful Annabel Lee:

For the moon never beams without bringing me dreams
    Of the beautiful Annabel Lee;
And the stars never rise, but I feel the bright eyes
    Of the beautiful Annabel Lee;
And so, all the night-tide, I lie down by the side
Of my darling—my darling—my life and my bride,
    In the sepulchre there by the sea,
    In her tomb by the sounding sea.

BIOGRAPHICAL RELEVANCE: As was mentioned in the last chapter, one should begin by asking in what ways the poem may be considered "advanced." To some readers, Poe's "Annabel Lee" seems fairly easy to understand and thus requires little analysis. The point is that on one level, the poem *is* relatively simple; in other ways and on other levels, however, the poem is extremely complex. To begin with, although it will not change one's understanding of the poem in any large way, one should at least know of the biographical elements behind it. Edgar Allan Poe married his cousin Virginia Clemm in 1836 when she was only thirteen years old. She died in 1847 when she was only twenty-four. It is usually supposed that she is the real

Annabel Lee and this makes clear certain lines like "I was a child and she was a child"; the implication is that she was literally a child and that Poe at least behaved and acted like a child. As a biographical utterance the poem acquires an even sadder—almost tragic—dimension.

EXPLAINING THE FAIRY-TALE MOTIF: Another question which should be asked, after clearly establishing the biographical possibilities, is, why does Poe choose to create a fairyland? He has deliberately composed a poem in the setting of a fairy-tale. Annabel Lee lived long, long ago in a kingdom by the sea— even though Poe wrote the poem shortly after his wife's death. The opening thus has the suggestion of "once upon a time there was a fairy princess, etc." Poe has chosen to present his sad story in the language of a fairy-tale in order to emphasize the unreality of his experience; by making the death of his wife similar to the death which occurs in a fairy-tale, Poe is able to avoid direct confrontation with the horrible reality implied by the death of someone beloved. His choice of the fairy-tale motif allows him to establish a distance from his subject; it makes something horrible and near (recent) seem instead pleasant and remote. The poem discusses beautiful love without morbid reference to the precise way in which the love was ended. Poe feels that the love continues, yet we feel his sense of uncertainty when he lies near his dead wife's tomb.

STYLISTIC DEVICES: SOUND PATTERNS, RHYME: Another question which needs to be asked is, how does Poe establish a pattern of sound which augments the narrated experience? In the arrangement of sounds Poe has managed to construct an elaborate system. Most effective is his use of repetition, which varies from a single word—as "many and many" in the first line—to whole phrases—as "In the kingdom by the sea." Notice too how many times Poe repeats the word "love." It is not simply a case of his trying to compare his love to that of others (the literal level), but rather also a case of his trying to saturate the world of the poem with a feeling of love. Poe uses love as a reason for his wife's death; the angels were jealous of the intensity and quality of the love experienced by the narrator and his Annabel Lee so they took her away from him. In other words, if she had to die, it was only because of the amount of love which she had. As with the establishment of a fairy-tale frame of reference, this serves to eliminate the basic unpleasant fact of premature death. Poe is trying to convince both himself and us that the death of a twenty-four-year-old girl in love can be beautiful. Through the strong rhyme sounds produced by the proliferation of words ending in "ee," Poe gives the poem a continuity. As the narrator speaks, the poem becomes increasingly rhythmic and thereby increasingly enchanting. This chanting, or enchanting use of rhyme, makes the fact of death even more remote. The sounds and the rhyme suggest the fairy world as much as the actual references to the kingdom by the sea. Everything in the poem converges on the idea of death in a melodious fashion so that when we read the rather macabre final stanza we are not the least bit shocked or even saddened. Because the poem is saturated with love and pleasant sounds, death itself is not frightening.

A STUDY IN CONTRASTS: Poe's poem provides a study in contrasts. We have the inherent, unstated contrast between Annabel Lee alive and dead. We have the image of the fruitful, peaceful, even magical kingdom by the sea juxtaposed with a cold cloud coming down out of the night bringing death. We have the brief suggestion of angels contrasted with devils, and of the poet's love contrasted with the love of those older and wiser than himself. The entire poem is based on the fundamental creation of a fairyland which is unique. Death does not come from angels' covetousness in fairy tales. Poe's fairyland, pieced together through both imagery and sound, is more complicated than it appears at first. But because of this delicate unreal structure, the love of the poet for Annabel, and her death, remain innocent and enchanting. And this is after all the effect which Poe wanted to achieve.

CASE 4: MARIANNE MOORE'S "THE MIND IS AN ENCHANTING THING"

THE MIND IS AN ENCHANTING THING
>   is an enchanted thing
>   like the glaze on a
>   katydid-wing
>   subdivided by sun
>   till the nettings are legion.

Like Gieseking playing Scarlatti;

like the apteryx-awl
  as a beak, or the
kiwi's rain-shawl
     of haired feathers, the mind
     feeling its way as though blind,
walks along with its eyes on the ground.

It has memory's ear
  that can hear without
having to hear.
  Like the gyroscope's fall,
  truly unequivocal
because trued by regnant certainty,

it is a power of
  strong enchantment. It
is like the dove-
     neck animated by
     sun; it is memory's eye;
it's conscientious inconsistency.

It tears off the veil; tears
  the temptation, the
mist the heart wears,
     from its eyes,—if the heart
     has a face; it takes apart
dejection. It's fire in the dove-neck's
iridescence, in the
  inconsistencies

of Scarlatti.
     Unconfusion submits
     its confusion to proof; it's
not a Herod's oath that cannot change.

EXPLAINING THE MOTIF OF ENCHANTMENT: From the opening thought, Marianne Moore's complex poem presents a two-dimensional world, for the mind is both enchanting and enchanted. In order to convey this double-enchantment, the poetess must somehow try to write in an enchanting way herself. And indeed she does; the delicacy of the glaze on a katydid-wing is by itself sufficient for establishing an enchanted world. But Miss Moore makes it even more enchanting by emphasizing the way in which it appears divided and sub-divided into sections by the sunlight; the netting suggests to her further enchanting things, such as Gieseking playing Scarlatti's music.

The poetess is attempting to suggest something about the mind which is indefinable. That is, the mind has certain capacities for experiencing which she is trying to evoke; the images shift sensuously, particularly as we envision an apteryx. Lest we leave anyone in confusion, an apteryx is a funny-looking bird, a kind of New Zealand kiwi; it has a long beak and does not fly; it is to birds what the anteater is in appearance to animals. The image of the mind groping along, flightless, like the apteryx borders on the comic but at the same time is highly suggestive. Furthermore, it establishes a large contrast between the winged, flying katydid and the unflying kiwi. The poem is attempting to suggest the paradoxes which one confronts when trying to describe the mind. Thus it flies but cannot fly; it is enchanted and enchanting; it hears but does not really need to hear. On the one hand it is unequivocal like the fall of a gyroscope, while on the other it exhibits inconsistency. Its unconfusion submits confusion, etc. In short, the entire poem is a delicate weaving of contrasts and opposites.

STYLISTIC DEVICES: THE USE OF DETAIL: The poem enchants the reader because of the delicacy with which details are introduced—witness the iridescence in the neck of the dove, the shawl formed on the kiwi by feathers, etc.—and because of the irregularity of rhyme, the interruption of ideas, and the sudden explosion of rhythm in the lines of abruptly changing lengths. Even the patterned line indentation serves to enchant us as our eyes move first inward and then out-ward. As we read the poem we feel ourselves turned into the pendulums of ticking clocks; we feel drenched in mystery and sunlight at the same time; we feel we are flying and we feel we are grounded. And, perhaps most importantly, we read in a cumulative way; we carry each image or suggestion with us as we move further into the poem. Stylistically Miss Moore is creating a poetic world right in front of us; we participate;

in short, we are enchanted. It is almost as if the poetess were forcing us to accept the opening premise that the mind is both an enchanting thing and an enchanted thing, for we witness the effects of someone else's concentration as we ourselves begin to concentrate. The katydid-wing becomes a picture rooted in our imagination—but put there by Marianne Moore rather than by ourselves.

As much of the paradox results from the sound as from the literal contradictions. The sound of "conscientious inconsistency" strikes the ear in a bizarre way. The same is true of other word-sound combinations, notably "iridescence, in the/ inconsistencies," "Unconfusion submits/ its confusion," etc. The "power of strong enchantment" rests in the mind because, in a final analysis, it is able to enchant itself. The mind involved in the entire imaginative process, as is the heart, and imagination is based on confusion. The poem challenges us and involves us at the same time; we respond through our forced participation, then carry on the process by ourselves without needing the stimulation of the poem. The details of the poem symbolize what is beautiful and what is possible; the style of the poem enforces the claimed enchantment, while the structure of the poem and the combination of sounds actually establish in us the capacity to be enchanted. The poem is thus unified in almost what might be called a magical way.

CASE 5: WILLIAM CARLOS WILLIAMS' "THE DANCE"

> In Breughel's great picture, The Kermess,
> the dancers go round, they go round and
> around, the squeal and the blare and the
> tweedle of bagpipes, a bugle and fiddles
> tipping their bellies, (round as the thick-
> sided glasses whose wash they impound)
> their hips and their bellies off balance
> to turn them. Kicking and rolling about
> the Fair Grounds, swinging their butts, those
> shanks must be sound to bear up under such
> rollicking measures, prance as they dance
> in Breughel's great picture, the Kermess.

PROBING THE LESS OBVIOUS: Sometimes a poet is able to crystallize a moment in an economical way, while at the same time making that moment seem like an eternity. Such is the case in William Carlos Williams' "The Dance." Having looked at a painting of a group of dancers, Williams apparently decided to reproduce the painting in words. A painting of course has no motion and thus it gives the student a chance to see how something inanimate can be animated. Williams has given life and vitality to what was still. Williams has enlarged the impact of the painting by presenting its underlying force. The question we must ask, is, *how* has the poet made the figures in the Breughel painting come alive?

STYLISTIC DEVICES: CREATING EFFECT OF MOTION: Williams' poem has a sustained atmosphere of motion. To begin with, the whole poem is only two sentences—that is, there is no long pause; everything flows evenly. In the second place the poem uses the same words more than once, as with "go round," or "bellies." The rhythm of the poem derives largely from the repetition of participles—tipping, kicking, rolling, swinging—and of sounds (alliteration)—"bagpipes, a bugle . . . bellies . . . bellies off balance . . . butts." The "b" sound is not simply repeated once, but instead recurs continuously once it has been introduced by the word blare. The bouncing "b" sound gives further sense of movement to the dancers. The entire poem is very delicately pieced together. Once Williams writes that the "dancers go round, they go round and/ around" we feel as if we are on a roller coaster and can not get off. Every sound, every word, every suggested movement—all put us together with the dancers in the painting. The different instruments—bagpipes, bugle, fiddles—and the different noises— squeal, blare, and tweedle—converge to make the poem musical. But we must notice how Williams has deliberately separated the instruments from their sounds; first he names all of the sounds in order to sweep us up in the music and action; then he mentions the instruments themselves, letting the movement of the fiddles lead into the movement of the bellies of the dancers. In this fashion there is an even greater correspondence between the dancers and the music than between the sounds and the instruments. The dancers themselves become a ringing sound and they "prance as they dance."

STRUCTURE AND MEANING: Through extremely tight control

over each word and each sound, and the exactly appropriate
positioning of each word and sound relative to the others,
Williams has created an explosive canvas. The style is so complex that it seems simple and thus the poem serves as a good
example of the way in which structure can enforce meaning
in a subtle way. The poem is "advanced" in its creation of
energetic rhythm through the ordinary tools of alliteration and
repetition. The force which Williams could detect beneath the
surface of the Breughel painting has been brought up to the
surface and made to leap out and engage the reader in a
highly exciting manner. In one sentence the poet has not only
captured the life-force of dancers but has captured the attention
and imagination of the reader as well.

CASE 6: ANDREW MARVELL'S "TO HIS COY MISTRESS"

> Had we but world enough, and time,
> This coyness, Lady, were no crime;
> We would sit down and think which way
> To walk and pass our long love's day.
> Thou by the Indian Ganges' side
> Shouldst rubies find: I by the tide
> Of Humber would complain. I would
> Love you ten years before the Flood,
> And you should, if you please, refuse
> Till the conversion of the Jews.
> My vegetable love should grow
> Vaster than empires, and more slow;
> An hundred years should go to praise
> Thine eyes and on thy forehead gaze;
> Two hundred to adore each breast,
> But thirty thousand to the rest;
> An age at least to every part,
> And the last age should show your heart.
> For, Lady, you deserve this state,
> Nor would I love at lower rate.
> But at my back I always hear
> Time's winged chariot hurrying near;
> And yonder all before us lie
> Deserts of vast eternity.
> Thy beauty shall no more be found,
> Nor, in thy marble vault, shall sound

My echoing song: then worms shall try
That long preserved virginity,
And your quaint honour turn to dust,
And into ashes all my lust:
The grave's a fine and private place,
But none, I think, do there embrace.
Now therefore, while the youthful hue
Sits on thy skin like morning dew,
And while thy willing soul transpires
At every pore with instant fires,
Now let us sport us while we may,
And now, like amorous birds of prey,
Rather at once our time devour
Than languish in his slow-chapt power.
Let us roll all our strength and all
Our sweetness up into one ball,
And tear our pleasures with rough strife
Through the iron gates of life:
Thus, though we cannot make our sun
Stand still, yet we will make him run.

ESTABLISHING BASIC MEANING: Marvell's poem, "To His Coy Mistress," is not only one of the best known seventeenth-century love poems in the metaphysical style, but one of the best poems in the English language. To understand its point of departure, one must be familiar with the fact that it is a variation on one of the most conventional themes of all literature: *carpe diem*. Meaning literally, "seize the day," a *carpe diem* poem always involves a poet's urging that his mistress or beloved take advantage of the present or, in other words, submit willingly to the poet's suggestion that they go off by themselves to make love. Seize the day; live for the present; why let time be wasted when there is so little of it? We are all growing older every day and we should enjoy youth to the fullest. This is the conventional approach taken by the writer of a *carpe diem* poem and Marvell is writing within the basic framework established by that convention.

STYLISTIC DEVICES: MIXING HUMOROUS AND SERIOUS: Marvell begins with a series of exaggerations introduced to make his plea more appealing; both world and time limit their possibilities for making love. It would be lovely to sit and think and walk, but there simply is not enough time for that luxury. Marvell imagines how coy the entire relationship could be; she could delay and he could keep pleading almost indefinitely. He would praise her again and again while she would not yield. One of the most striking facts about Marvell's poem is that we discover a blend of humor with serious love-statement. That is, the opening hyperboles are as comic as they are urgent, as hilarious as they are honest. Stylistically it is very difficult to establish this blend and thus Marvell's composition is relatively advanced. For example, the second section of the poem moves away from the humorous references to his mistress's body in the closing of the first section. In these opening lines of the second section we find some very beautiful poetry; these lines could easily occur in a poem wholly serious; they suggest the infinity of love and emphasize perfectly the limits of mortality:

>   But at my back I always hear
>   Time's winged chariot hurrying near;
>   And yonder all before us lie
>   Deserts of vast eternity.

In these lines, Marvell adds logic to his already logical appeal; as they are mortals, desirous of enjoying mortal love, they must, logically, express and partake of that love now, for soon they will no longer even be mortals. Notice how the tone of this serious logic suddenly returns again to a humorous attitude as Marvell imagines worms trying his lady's carefully guarded virginity. While the tone has shifted, the logic is still strong: she might as well let the poet have her virginity because the worms will only have it later. The humor is punctuated perfectly by the couplet which ends the second section of the poem, "The grave's a fine and private place,/ But none, I think, do there embrace." Marvell knows that his appeal will be best if it yokes together cold logic and flirtatious wit; and these two facets of his appeal are the central facets of the poem's development.

LOGICAL RESOLUTION: The third section of the poem emphasizes at last the necessity of action. "Now" Marvell repeatedly asserts is the time; he writes, "Now therefore," "Now let us sport," and "now, like amorous birds," etc. Marvell indulges in the kind of flattery and exaggeration which he ridiculed in the opening of the poem; he wants the reader to realize his awareness of the necessity for his duplicity. His humor takes the bite out of his hypocrisy. The basic logic is that the narrator and his love should beat time at his own game; they should devour time rather than let time devour them (the word "slow-chapt" means slowly devouring, or slow-jawed). Time must not only be used now, but conquered now as well. The ending of the poem is an explosive and ambiguous image; the poet urges that his mistress join with him in rolling all of their sweetness up into one ball, etc., and we are not sure whether this ball in fact becomes their sun, or whether simply the sun will run, that is, time will fly, as they enter into love. The latter interpretation seems more appropriate in light of the preceding lines. The poet has urged that they conquer time; making the sun run would be an expression of time's flying in retreat from the force of their violent love-making. The poet thus flatters the possibilities of their love as well as the mistress herself. The corollary logic is simply that the lady is beautiful, yes, but that beauty is small in comparison with the beauty of their possible love; all that is required is the lady's consent.

EVALUATING THE POEM:　　Marvell has treated a familiar theme with great imagination; through a sophisticated, light and racy combination of playfulness and aggression, his preferred love and wooing are seen both seriously and humorously. His logic is incisive because time is indeed always passing. Marvell's innovation arrives primarily in his use of the idea that they not only act now but that they *conquer* now; time will not merely be ignored—it will be defeated. This aspect of the poet's logic, carved out meticulously in couplets of iambic tetrameter, presents a new kind of challenge to a lady probably already used to resisting mere flattery. The poem is thus very polished and persuasive enough, probably, to be a successful example of its kind.

CASE 7: RALPH WALDO EMERSON'S "EACH AND ALL"

> Little thinks, in the field, yon red-cloaked clown
> Of thee from the hilltop looking down;
> The heifer that lows in the upland farm,
> Far-heard, lows not thine ear to charm;
> The sexton, tolling his bell at noon,
> Deems not that great Napoleon

Stops his horse, and lists with delight,
Whilst his files sweep round yon Alpine height;
No knowest thou what argument
Thy life to thy neighbor's creed has lent.
All are needed by each one;
Nothing is fair or good alone.
I thought the sparrow's note from heaven,
Singing at dawn on the alder bough;
I brought him home, in his nest, at even;
He sings the song, but it cheers not now,
For I did not bring home the river and sky;—
He sang to my ear,—they sang to my eye.
The delicate shells lay on the shore;
The bubbles of the latest wave
Fresh pearls to their enamel gave,
And the bellowing of the savage sea
Greeted their safe escape to me.
I wiped away the weeds and foam,
I fetched my sea-born treasures home;
But the poor, unsightly, noisome things
Had left their beauty on the shore
With the sun and the sand and the wild uproar.
The lover watched his graceful maid,
As 'mid the virgin train she strayed,
Nor knew her beauty's best attire
Was woven still by the snow-white choir.
At last she came to his hermitage,
Like the birds from the woodlands to the cage;—
The gay enchantment was undone,
A gentle wife, but fairy none.
Then I said, "I covet truth;
Beauty is unripe childhood's cheat;
I leave it behind with the games of youth."—
As I spoke, beneath my feet
The ground pine curled its pretty wreath,
Running over the club moss burs;
I inhaled the violet's breath;
Around me stood the oaks and firs;
Pine cones and acorns lay on the ground;
Over me soared the eternal sky,
Full of light and of diety;
Again I say, again I heard,

The rolling river, the morning bird;—
Beauty through my senses stole;
I yielded myself to the perfect whole.

ESTABLISHING BASIC MEANING: Emerson's poem is formed
of a series of parallels and analogies. Through tightly controlled
logic Emerson has presented the results of his experience *of* and
in nature. He works through his own experiments with us in
order to demonstrate the truth and accuracy of his conclusions.
Emerson's central idea is that examples of the beauty of nature
can not be isolated and maintain their beauty. Nature is beautiful precisely *because* things are dependent on each other for
continuing beauty. What Emerson realizes, now that he is older,
is that one can not experience nature in a fragmented way; one
must be willing to absorb an entire set of surroundings rather
than absorb only part of them. Emerson is trying to demonstrate the existence of "the perfect whole"; that is, he is trying to
explain his conclusion that beauty depends on the unity of all
things. But within that unity every creature or plant or object
must go its own way without full awareness of being a part
of something larger. The truth about life is that each of its
parts does not always concern itself with all of the rest of the
parts; by functioning independently they create a perfect, united
whole. The scarecrow does not think about man, anymore
than the bellowing heifer thinks to bellow in order to please
some distant ear. Few people realize that something happening
in their life will have an effect on their neighbor's life. Emerson's
central idea is presented in the couplet: "All are needed by
each one;/ Nothing is fair or good alone."

THE TECHNIQUE OF PARALLEL EXAMPLES: In order to demonstrate the truth of this idea, Emerson explains how he first took
home a sparrow he had heard singing on an alder bough.
When he has the bird home and listens to its song, he realizes
that its beauty depends partially on the setting in which he had
first seen the bird singing; the poet's "problem" is that he
had not also brought home the river and the sky. Only one of
his senses—auditory—was being stimulated; he needs to be
able to see the beauty as well as listen to it. There is a very
delicate sensory experience here in which in order for one
sense to be satisfied, all must be satisfied.

Parallel to this first failure is a second one in which the poet explains how he saw some "delicate shells" lying on the shore, being washed by the breaking waves. He wiped off the foam and weeds and took the shells home, only to realize that they did not seem as pretty without the sound of the sea nearby; they are "noisome," that is, offensive to the sense of smell or other of the senses; they are "unsightly." The problem is that they "Had left their beauty on the shore/ With the sun and the sand and the wild uproar." In order to be beautiful, the shells must be in their natural environment; removed from that environment they are not only not beautiful, but even repulsive. As with the attempt to take the beauty of the bird home, the attempt to take the beauty of the sea-shells home has also failed.

In a third and parallel example, the poet explains how a lover marries a beautiful woman and she is no longer possessed of her virginal beauty. She goes to his hermitage "Like the bird from the woodlands to the cage." Emerson has thus used the analogy as a simile; the example functions both logically and figuratively. In three separate but parallel cases, the poet has observed that beauty is not lasting; he expresses his disappointment and suggests that beauty is nothing more than a cheat of unripe childhood. But as he speaks he looks at the ground and is impressed by the unity of a scene in nature. He sees the ground below, the sky above, and the light; he breathes in the fresh smell of the violet; he hears the rolling of a river and the song of a bird. There is almost a bombardment of all his senses; he is seeing, smelling, and listening to beauty; thus he writes, "Beauty through my senses stole;/ I yielded myself to the perfect whole."

SUMMARY AND EVALUATION: Through a series of logically parallel examples, Emerson has poetically demonstrated the truth of his feeling that beauty is a unified appeal to all of the senses. No one can isolate a bird for only its song; no one can simply look at shells sitting at home; no one can marry a girl and expect her to maintain her virginal beauty. Unspoiled nature means just that! Emerson has successfully woven together a wide collection of sensory stimuli; we, as readers, have felt the unity of sensual beauty; we have seen the curling ground pine, smelled the violet, and heard the sound of the bird singing in the morning. We have participated in the futility of attempting to isolate and fragment beauty into parts. Emerson has succeeded in convincing us of an idea; he has made simple what could be considered a relatively complex truth.

CONCLUSION

In our attempt to broaden our understanding of poetry we have discussed in varying degrees of "depth" the poems of eighteen English poets—Arnold, Browning, Byron, Coleridge, Davies, Donne, Dryden, Herbert, Keats, Marvell, Masefield, Pope, Shakespeare, Swinburne, Tennyson, Vaughan, and Wordsworth —and of thirteen American poets—Auden, Dickinson, Emerson, Frost, Millay, Moore, Poe, Ransom, Robinson, Stevens, Williams, Wylie. In every poem we have discovered problems; in some cases we have solved them, in others we have made an educated attempt at solution, and in others we have bowed to the mystery in the poet's private world.

ANALYZING POETRY IS ASKING QUESTIONS: If there is any one lesson in this book which can be singled out for maximum importance, it is, simply, that the analysis of poetry is really the process of asking questions. Further, we must ask the right kind of questions and the right number of questions. There is no denying that unlimited questioning can sweep one far away into unspeculative idiocy; therefore it is of great importance to know not only where to begin, but when to stop, as well. When analyzing any poem, the reader should realize that his first task is to read the poem several times. Successive readings usually sharpen not only one's understanding of the poem, but one's capacity to ask questions. The more familiar one becomes with a poem, the more easily one will be able to formulate questions.

IMPORTANCE OF TERMINOLOGY: Basic to all analysis is the collection of literary terms used in the discussion of poetry; there is no substitute for familiarity with the language of criticism as a primary prerequisite of the process of criticism. When one begins with a sound understanding of meter, rhyme, and rhythm, and then adds the critical vocabulary which includes words like allegory, alliteration, archetype, bathos, cacophony, and euphemism, one is then able to approach poems with a readiness to respond in writing. The technical framework within which one must present critical writings is, in a way, a useful and simplifying tool. Having "rules" eliminates certain decisions of both taste and convention.

ESTABLISHED APPROACHES: Having certain approaches which are established and accepted strengthens one's ability to communicate the ideas which one has about a particular poem; whether the critic's approach is objective or subjective, thematic or historical, doctrinal or aesthetic, one is given direction by the mere choice of that approach which dictates certain necessary references to aspects of the poem. While the main task of the critic is to ask questions, knowing the techniques of analysis makes it easier for the critic to answer those questions. Thus in the analysis of poetry, in the actual process of taking a poem apart in order to arrive at a greater understanding of its structure and meaning, the critic is relying on both subjective response and objective ability to communicate the nature of, and reasons for, that response.

MAKING ANALYSIS CORRESPOND TO THE COMPLEXITIES OF THE POEM: In differentiating between analysis and advanced analysis it should be clear by now that we are only differentiating between poetry which is not difficult to understand and more complex poetry. Further, we are actually differentiating among our different capacities for discussing a poem without becoming trite. Analysis should correspond to the poem being analyzed; thus the critic should decide at the outset the extent to which he is both willing and able to carry his discussion. Literary style can be one of the most puzzling complexities facing the critic. Symbolism and questions of literary indebtedness involve the reader in the dimension of analysis similar to detective work. Sophistication must be equalled by sophistication; critics must live up to the complexity of a poem without feeling that by so doing they will lose any of the great pleasure which we all can experience in analyzing poetry.

BIBLIOGRAPHY AND GUIDE
TO FURTHER RESEARCH

Barnet, Sylvan, with M. Berman and W. Burto. *A Dictionary of Literary Terms.* Boston: Little, Brown and Co., 1960. This book constitutes a lengthier list than the one presented here and is a very useful "handbook" for readers of poetry.

Thrall, Hibbard, and Holman. *A Handbook to Literature.* New York: The Odyssey Press, 1960. This handbook is much longer than the one listed above and thus has more entries; however, there are more detailed references than the average student of poetry would require. To graduate students and others who want to pursue advanced study of literature, it is essential.

Richards, I. A. *Practical Criticism; A Study of Literary Judgement.* New York: Harcourt, Brace & World, Inc. (originally published in 1929); re-issued as a Harvest Book paperback (H. B. 16). A very useful demonstration of ways in which one can discuss poetry; particularly useful with reference to problems in meter and rhyme.

Bodkin, Maud. *Archetypal Patterns in Poetry; Psychological Studies of Imagination.* New York: Random House (a Vintage Book), 1958. A psychological treatment of various literary archetypes which recur throughout literature.

Bradley, A. C. *Oxford Lectures on Poetry.* Bloomington: Indiana University Press, 1961. A celebrated series of lectures on particular aspects of poetry and poetic criticism; particularly useful to the student interested in Shakespeare or Shelley.

Johnson, Samuel. *Lives of the Poets*. There are many editions. Johnson's thoughts on poets and their poems are lively and interesting; anyone interested in writing casually in a "chatty" way about poems should first read some of Johnson's essays; his "Life of Milton" is particularly good.

There are innumerable examples of literary questioning and literary analysis. The reader is encouraged to examine some of the articles appearing in the journals of literary criticism.

There are several good anthologies of poetry for single periods of literature and innumerable ones covering several periods. The four which I have found particularly useful and enjoyable are the following:

Coffin, Charles M. *The Major Poets: English and American*. Harcourt, Brace & World, Inc., 1954.

Quiller-Couch, Arthur. *The Oxford Book of English Verse*. Oxford: at the Clarendon Press, 1924.

Williams, Oscar. *The Pocket Book of Modern Verse*. New York: Washington Square Press, 1958.

Williams, Oscar and Honig, Edwin. *The Mentor Book of Major American Poets*. New York: Mentor Books, 1962.

INDEX

NOTES

NOTES

NOTES